CW0068856Ə

DISCERNING TRUTH

Exposing Errors in
Evolutionary Arguments

Dr. Jason Lisle

First printing: July 2010

Copyright © 2010 by Jason Lisle. All rights reserved. No part of this book may be used or reproduced in any manner whatsoever without written permission of the publisher, except in the case of brief quotations in articles and reviews. For information write:
Master Books®, P.O. Box 726, Green Forest, AR 72638
Master Books is a division of the New Leaf Publishing Group, Inc.

ISBN: 978-0-89051-594-5
Library of Congress Number: 2010929901

Cover by Diana Bogardus

Unless otherwise noted, all Scripture is from the New American Standard Bible.

Printed in the United States of America

Please visit our website for other great titles:
www.masterbooks.net

For information regarding author interviews,
please contact the publicity department at (870) 438-5288.

Master
Books®
A Division of New Leaf Publishing Group
www.masterbooks.net

Contents

Preface

In my previous book, *The Ultimate Proof of Creation*, I included two chapters that gave brief summaries of the nature of logic and examples of common logical fallacies as they occur in debates on origins. Initially, I was somewhat reluctant to include these chapters because I was concerned that they might read a bit like stale dictionary entries and possibly break the flow of thought that permeated the rest of the book. But ultimately, I decided that knowledge of logical fallacies is simply too important to be left out of a book on defending the Christian faith. Shortly after the book was published, I was astounded at the number of people who wrote to me or told me in person how much they appreciated the book — how it had changed their entire approach to apologetics (defending the faith) and had given them a new boldness to share their faith. In particular, I was surprised by the number of people who told me how much they appreciated the chapters on logic.

Encouraged by this initial feedback, as well as positive responses from talks I had given on logical fallacies and evolution, I decided that a more thorough treatment of the subject was in order. But I didn't want to write just another "textbook" on logic; there are plenty of those in print already. Nor did I want to simply repeat the short summaries that I had already written for *The Ultimate Proof*. Rather, I wanted to produce a resource on logic in apologetics, written in a way that is engaging and memorable, perhaps using anecdotes from my own experiences in apologetics. Moreover, I wanted to spend a considerable amount of space on each fallacy (at least for the more common ones), so that the reader thoroughly understands each example before moving on to the next.

This led me to write a short series of articles on logical fallacies that we posted on the Answers in Genesis website (answersingenesis.org). Each article addresses one fallacy (or perhaps two at most). This format allows the reader to absorb the information in a very readable and (hopefully) entertaining way, with illustrations and examples from my own experiences. The series concentrated on fallacies that are commonly committed by evolutionists as they attempt to defend their position. I am convinced that evolution is without any intellectual merit whatsoever, and that all arguments for evolution are either logically fallacious, or based on a false premise. So I was curious to see how the evolutionists would respond to the web series since it revealed the fallacious nature of some of their most cherished arguments.

And respond they did! Internet blogs and forums exploded with angry evolutionists attempting to rebut, ridicule, or simply dismiss the fallacy series. Ironically, most of their responses contained the very fallacies that had already been refuted in the series. Such responses indicate that we have struck a nerve. After all, without logical fallacies, how would evolutionists defend their position? But don't take my word for it. In chapter 14 of this book, we have numerous examples of fallacies directly from evolutionary literature, along with references that you may check for yourself.

This book is based on that web series. However, I have added additional material in a number of places. First of all, I have added five

8

brand-new chapters. I have also made minor changes and additions to the previously published chapters, which I believe will close most of the loopholes, and clarify some ambiguity that may have appeared in the web versions. Since the web series included only the most common fallacies, I have added a new chapter to this book that covers almost all the other fallacies that occur in origins debates. Since these are less common, I felt that they warranted less space, and so only a brief description and example for each is given.

The most exciting new additions to this book (in my view at least) are chapters 12–15. Chapter 12 includes assorted examples of fallacies from all the types included in this book. This allows the reader to test his or her fallacy-detection skills. An answer key is provided in chapter 13. Chapter 14 has another list of assorted examples of evolutionist fallacies quoted directly from evolutionist literature — along with references. Since these are "real world" examples, they may be more difficult to classify than the hypothetical, chemically pure examples provided in chapter 12. An answer key is also provided in chapter 15, which includes an explanation of why each fallacy is classified as such. Sometimes fallacies are called by their Latin name, or have an alternative English name. Therefore, I have included appendix A, which gives alternate names used for logical fallacies.

This book is not meant to be a replacement for a textbook on logic. Many fine textbooks (such as Copi and Cohen's *Introduction to Logic*) are available. Rather, this book is designed to supplement other such material. It focuses almost exclusively on how to spot and refute fallacies that occur in evolutionists' arguments. This is an important aspect of apologetics. But it is not the only aspect. Defending the faith requires knowledge of the faith and how to critique alternative worldviews. Books such as *The Ultimate Proof of Creation* and *The New Answers Book* series are designed to give a more encompassing picture of how to defend the Christian faith, particularly in Genesis. However, I am convinced that knowing logic and learning to spot logical fallacies in order to defend the faith better is one of the most valuable time investments that a person can make.

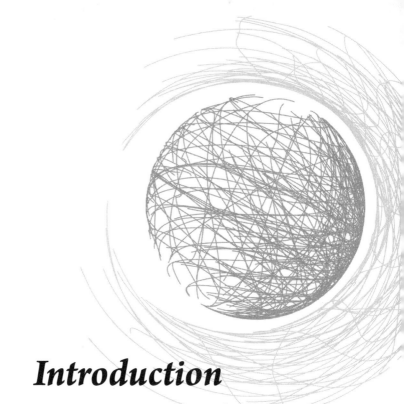

Introduction

Whenever I hear people debating some issue (abortion, gun control, origins, religion, politics, etc.), I often spot a number of mistakes in their arguments. Mistakes in reasoning are called "logical fallacies," and they abound in origins debates. I have often thought it would be fun to carry a little buzzer that I could push when someone makes a fundamental mistake in reasoning. Of course, that would be impolite. However, we should all become familiar with logical fallacies so that our mental buzzer goes off whenever we hear a mistake in reasoning.

Logic (the study of correct and incorrect reasoning) has become a lost skill in our culture. And that is a shame. It is a very valuable tool, particularly for the Christian who wants to defend his or her faith better. Evolutionists often commit logical fallacies, and it is important that creationists learn to identify and refute such faulty reasoning. Sadly, I often see creationists committing logical fallacies as well. There is hardly anything more embarrassing than someone who advocates your position, but does so using bad reasoning!

Logic involves the use of arguments. When some people think of "arguments," they think of an emotionally heated exchange — a "yelling match." But that is not what is meant here. An argument is a chain of statements (called "propositions") in which the truth of one is asserted on the basis of the other(s). Biblically, we are supposed to argue in this way; we are to provide a reasoned defense (an argument) for the Christian faith (1 Pet. 3:15) with gentleness and respect. An argument takes certain information as accepted (this is called a "premise"), and then proceeds to demonstrate that another claim must also be true (called the "conclusion"). Here is an example:

> Dr. Lisle is not in the office today. So he is probably working at home.

In this argument, the first sentence is the premise: "Dr. Lisle is not in the office today." The arguer has assumed that we all agree to this premise and then draws the conclusion that "he is probably working at home." This is a reasonable argument; the conclusion does seem likely, given the premise. So this is called a "cogent" argument. This type of argument is classified as an *inductive* argument because the conclusion is likely, but not proved, from the premise. (After all, Dr. Lisle could be on vacation.) If the conclusion were *not* very likely given the premise, then the argument would be considered "weak" rather than "cogent."

The other type of argument is called a *deductive* argument. With this type of argument, it is asserted that the conclusion *definitely* follows from the premises (not just *probably*). For example:

> All dogs are mammals. And all mammals have hair. Therefore, all dogs have hair.

The conclusion of this argument definitely follows from the premises. That is, if the premises are true, then the conclusion has to be true as well. So this is a *valid* argument. If the conclusion did not follow for a deductive argument, then the argument would be *invalid*.

Over the next chapters, we will explore the most common logical fallacies. It is very helpful to know these fallacies so that we can spot them when evolutionists commit them — and so that we do not commit them as well. In the Christian worldview, to be logical is to think in a way that is consistent with God's thinking. God is logical.

As Christians, we have a moral obligation to think and act rationally — to line up our thinking with God's truth (Eph. 5:1; Isa. 55:7–8). I pray that this book will be God-honoring and will tremendously improve your defense of the faith.

Key — can you draw this △ from this premise/proposition (does it follow?) look for the GAP between the two!

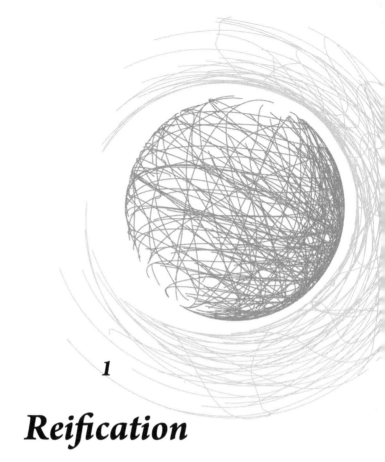

1

Reification

Reification[1] is attributing a concrete characteristic to something that is abstract. Perhaps you have heard the old saying, "It's not nice to fool Mother Nature." This is an example of reification because "nature" is an abstraction; it is simply the name we give to the chain of events in the universe. Nature is not a person and cannot literally be fooled, since nature does not have a mind. So this expression would not make sense if taken literally.

Of course, not all language should be taken literally. There is nothing wrong with reification as a figure of speech. It is perfectly acceptable in poetry. Even the Bible uses reification at times in its poetic sections. For example, Proverbs 8 personifies the concept of wisdom. This is a perfectly acceptable (and poetically beautiful) use of reification.

However, when reification is used as part of a *logical argument,* it is a fallacy. The reason for this is that using such a poetic expression is often ambiguous and can obscure important points in a debate. It is very common for evolutionists to commit this fallacy. Let's look at some examples of the *fallacy of reification* as they are commonly used in evolutionary arguments.

> *Reification*
> —
> *attributing*
> *a concrete*
> *characteristic*
> *to something*
> *abstract*

Sometimes in an argument, an evolutionist will say something like this: "*Nature* has designed some amazing creatures." This sentence commits the fallacy of reification because nature does not have a mind and cannot literally design anything. By using the fallacy of reification, the evolutionist obscures the fact that the evolution worldview really cannot account for the design of living creatures. (Keep in mind that he may be doing this unintentionally.) God can design creatures because God is a supernatural being. Nature is a concept and cannot design anything.

"Creationists say the world was created supernaturally, but *science* says otherwise." Here the person has attributed personal, concrete attributes to the concept of *science*. In doing so, he or she overlooks the important fact that *scientists* draw conclusions about the evidence and verbalize such conclusions — not "science." Science is a conceptual tool that can be used properly or improperly. It says nothing. It does not take a position on issues. So this common example of reification is logically fallacious.

"The *evidence* speaks for itself." This expression is quite common, but when used as part of an argument, it is the fallacy of reification. Evidence does not speak at all. Evidence is a concept: the name we give to a body of facts that we believe to be consistent with a particular point of view. People draw conclusions about evidence and verbalize their thoughts. But evidence itself does not have thoughts to verbalize.

"*Evolution* figured out a way around these problems." I have heard a number of evolutionists say something along these lines when attempting to explain some intricately designed biological system. But, of

course, evolution is a concept. It has no mind and cannot figure out anything. So this example again obscures the difficulty in accounting for design in the universe without appealing to a mind. It is a fallacious use of reification.

Even the phrase *natural selection* is an example of reification and could be considered a fallacy, if used in an argument. Nature cannot literally select. This phrase is so commonly used that we might not call it a fallacy, providing the meaning is understood by all. We do believe in the concept called "natural selection." Yes, organisms that are well-suited to an environment are more likely to survive than those that are not well-suited. (This is tautologically true, a statement always considered correct, and is something that both creationists and evolutionists believe.)

But suppose we asked, "Why is it that animals are well-suited to their environment?" If an evolutionist answered "natural selection," this would be the fallacy of reification. It poetically obscures the true reason that animals are designed to survive — God.

If you think about it, natural selection does not actually explain why we find organisms suited to their environment. It only explains why we do *not* find organisms that are *unsuited* to their environment (i.e., because they die). It is God — not "nature" — who has given living beings the abilities they need to survive.

Often the concept being reified is given personal characteristics: the ability to think, to have an opinion, and so on. When concepts are personified in this way in an argument, it is sometimes called the "pathetic fallacy." The term is not pejorative; rather, it comes from the word *empathy*, because we are attributing thoughts and feelings to something that cannot possess them. So the pathetic fallacy is a type of reification. Virtually all of the examples above could also be classified as the pathetic fallacy. Usually, the personification of non-conceptual objects is also classified as the pathetic fallacy (if it occurs within an argument). The statement "Cars really want to be driven" would be considered the pathetic fallacy if it occurred in an argument, even though cars are not conceptual but physical.

Examples of Reification

"Nature has found a way."

"Life invaded the dry land."

"Natural selection guided the development of this species."

"Science says that we must limit explanations to the natural world."

"Follow the evidence where it leads."

"Evolution tells us much about the way the world works."

Endnotes
1. Reification is also commonly called "hypostatization."

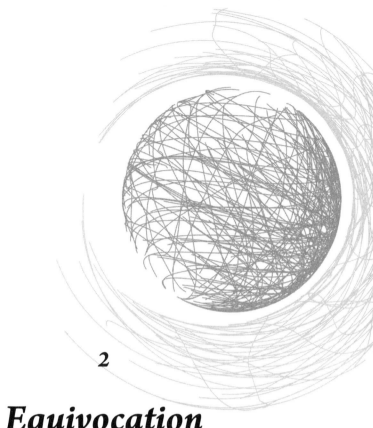

2

Equivocation

When debating on any topic, it is very important that we pay close attention to the meaning of words and how they are being used in the debate. Most words have a range of possible meanings, but only one of these meanings will properly fit the given context. When someone shifts from one meaning of a word to another within an argument, he or she has committed the fallacy of equivocation.

Here is a facetious example: "Doctors know a lot about medicine, and Dr. Lisle is a doctor. So he must know a lot about medicine." This short argument shifts from one meaning of the word *doctor* (medical doctor) to another (Ph.D.), making the argument fallacious. This use of equivocation is sometimes called a "bait and switch" fallacy because the listener is baited on one meaning of a word, and then the meaning is switched to draw a faulty conclusion.

Evolutionists often commit the fallacy of equivocation on the word *evolution*. This word has a number of meanings. *Evolution* can mean "change" in a general sense, but it can also refer to the idea that organisms share a common ancestor. Either meaning is perfectly legitimate, but the two meanings should not be conflated within an argument. Many evolutionists seem to think that by demonstrating evolution in the sense of "change," it somehow proves evolution in the sense of "common descent."

You might hear them say something like, "Creationists are wrong because we can see evolution happening all the time. Organisms are constantly changing and adapting to their environment." But, of course, the fact that animals change does not demonstrate that they share a common ancestor.

I cannot overstate how common this fallacy is in evolutionary arguments. Bacteria becoming resistant to antibiotics, speciation events, changes in the size and shape of finch beaks, the development of new breeds of dog, and changes in allele frequency are all examples of *change*, but none of them demonstrate that the basic kinds of organisms share a common ancestor. When you hear evolutionists cite these as examples of "evolution in action," you need to politely point out that they have committed the fallacy of equivocation.

You might notice that at Answers in Genesis we often use phrases like "particles-to-people evolution." This may seem overly cumbersome, but we do this precisely to avoid equivocation.

Another word on which people sometimes equivocate is the word *science*. *Science* commonly

> *Equivocation*
> —
> *shifting from one meaning of a word to another within an argument*

refers to the procedures by which we explore the consistent and predictable behavior of the universe today — the scientific method. This is operational science. But *science* can also refer to a body of knowledge (e.g., the science of genetics). Furthermore, *science* can also refer to models regarding past events; this is origins science. Or it can refer to a specific model. When any of these meanings are switched within an argument, it is an instance of the fallacy of equivocation.

"Science has given us computers, medicine, the space program, and so much more. Why then do you deny the science of evolution?" This argument merges operational science with one particular model of origins science. Origins science lacks the testable, repeatable aspects of operational science because the past can never be tested directly, nor repeated. Computers, medicine, and so on are all an outworking of operational science (the study of how the universe operates today).

By merging operational science with evolution, the arguer hopes to give evolution a credibility that it does not truly deserve. Yes, we do believe in operational science, and we have some respect for origins science as well. However, this does not mean that we should believe in evolution — which is only one particular model of origins science.

Old-earth creationists often commit this fallacy on the word *interpretation*. They may say, "We must always compare our interpretation of Scripture with our interpretation of nature." Interpretation of the Scripture means to understand the meaning of the propositional statements — to grasp the author's intention. However, nature does not have intentions.

When we interpret nature, we are *creating* propositional statements about nature. This is very different than understanding propositional statements that someone else has already created. By merging these two meanings of *interpretation,* the old-earth creationist places scientists' statements about nature on the same level as Scripture.

Examples of Equivocation

"Science is a very powerful tool, so why deny the science of evolution?"

"Evolution is a scientific fact. The evolution of bacteria becoming resistant is well-documented."

"We don't deny the Bible, but it's your interpretation we believe to be wrong. We must always compare our interpretation of the Bible with our interpretation of nature to make sure they match."

"The science that put men on the moon is the same kind of science we use to study what happened millions of years ago. You don't deny the one, so why deny the other?"

"Species are constantly evolving — adapting to their environment. The evolution of the SARS virus, the changes in allele frequency of many organisms, and the various breeds of dog all demonstrate the truth of evolution. How can creationists honestly deny evolution?"

NB! To disguise equivocation one might use a synonym to make it less obvious!

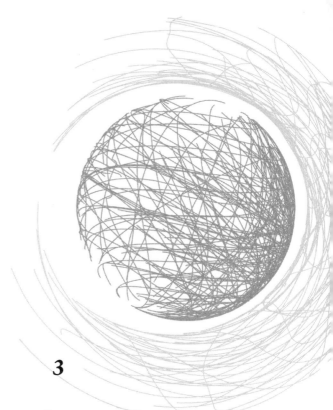

3

Begging the Question

(I'm an atheist because I don't believe in God)
circular

I once did a telescope session with a small group of people, including a four-year-old boy who was particularly interested in astronomy. I asked this young budding astronomer if he believed in alien spaceships. "Of course," he said. I then asked him *why* he believed in alien spaceships. I'll never forget his clever response: "How else would the aliens get here?" Pretty logical, isn't it? The aliens would never be able to get to earth without a spaceship. So, clearly, there must be alien spaceships!

This is a wonderful example of a very common error in reasoning — the fallacy of begging the question. This fallacy is committed when a person merely assumes what he or she is attempting to prove, or when the premise of an argument actually depends upon its conclusion. In this

a roof doesn't support an house

case, our young student was attempting to prove the existence of alien spacecraft by taking it for granted that aliens have traveled to earth. But that is essentially the point in question. This young aspiring astronomer was reasoning in a circle.

Of course, we expect such humorous reasoning from a four year old. As we grow up, we are expected to become rational and not make these kinds of logical mistakes. That's why it is so disturbing to find that many adults commit the fallacy of begging the question in debates on origins. Some examples are obvious: "Evolution must be true because it is a fact." But, more commonly, the fallacy is much more subtle. Consider some of the following arguments.

"The Bible cannot be true because it contains miracles, and miracles violate the laws of nature!"

Yes, miracles can potentially involve a temporary suspension of the laws of nature (not that all of them necessarily do).[1] Since the Bible makes it clear that God is beyond natural laws, He can suspend them if He wishes to. But the critic's argument has simply taken it for granted that violations of the laws of nature are impossible. In other words, the arguer has already assumed that the Bible is false — in order to argue that the Bible is false. He has begged the question.

You may have heard people argue: "The Bible cannot be true because it teaches that the earth is only thousands of years old; whereas, we know the earth is billions of years old."

> *Begging the question*
>
> —
>
> *merely assuming what one is attempting to prove*

All such arguments commit the fallacy of begging the question. Here is why. Old earth arguments are all based on the assumptions of naturalism (nature is all that there is) and a large degree of uniformitarianism (present rates and processes are representative of past rates and processes). Then, by extrapolating from present rates of various earth processes, the person estimates how long it would take to build up or erode certain geological features or how long it would take for a radioisotope to decay.

assserted as true but is yet to be proven

But the Bible denies naturalism and uniformitarianism (e.g., erosion rates during the global Flood). By assuming naturalism and uniformitarianism, the critic has already merely assumed that the Bible is wrong. He then uses this assumption to conclude that the Bible is wrong. His reasoning is circular.

"Creation cannot be true because you would have to ignore all that scientific evidence."

But this argument begs the question because it presupposes that scientific evidence somehow provides support for evolution, which has not been demonstrated.

"It makes no sense to deny evolution; it is a well-established fact of nature."

This argument also begs the question since the truth status of evolution is the very question at issue.

Christians are not always above circular reasoning either. Some have argued, "The Bible must be the Word of God because it says it is. And what it says must be true, since God cannot lie."

Of course, it is quite true that the Bible does claim to be the Word of God (2 Tim. 3:16; Rom. 10:17), and it is also true that God does not lie (Titus 1:2). But when one of these statements is used as the sole support for the other, the argument commits the fallacy of begging the question. The same line of argumentation could be used to "prove" the Koran, which of course we would deny.

Now it's time to get a little philosophically deep. Brace yourself. Begging the question is a very strange fallacy because it is actually *valid*. Recall that a valid argument is one in which the conclusion does follow from the premises. Normally, fallacies are not valid; the fact that their conclusion does not follow from the premise(s) is what makes them fallacies. But oddly, with begging the question the conclusion does follow from the premise (because it is simply a restatement of the premise). So the argument, "Evolution must be true because it is a fact," is valid. But if it is valid, then why is it considered a fallacy?

The answer would seem to be that begging the question is a fallacy because it is *arbitrary*. Circular arguments of this kind are not useful because anyone who denies the conclusion would also deny the premise (since the conclusion is essentially the same as the premise). So the argument, "Evolution must be true because it is a fact," while technically valid, is fallacious because the arguer has merely assumed what he is trying to prove.

Arbitrary assumptions are not to be used in logical reasoning because we could equally well assume the exact opposite. It would be just as legitimate to argue, "Evolution cannot be true because it is false."

It should be noted that there are certain special cases where circular reasoning is unavoidable and not necessarily fallacious. Since begging the question is valid and is only considered a fallacy because it is arbitrary, we should consider cases where it is not arbitrary. There are some situations where the conclusion of an argument must be assumed at the outset by anyone participating in the debate.[2] Here is an example:

an assertion

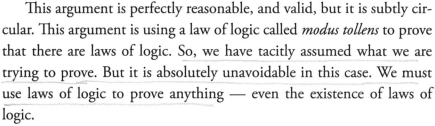

1. Without laws of logic, we could not make a valid argument.
2. We can make a valid argument.
3. Therefore, there must be laws of logic.

This argument is perfectly reasonable, and valid, but it is subtly circular. This argument is using a law of logic called *modus tollens* to prove that there are laws of logic. So, we have tacitly assumed what we are trying to prove. But it is absolutely unavoidable in this case. We must use laws of logic to prove anything — even the existence of laws of logic.

However, the above argument is not arbitrary. We do have a good reason for assuming laws of logic, since without them we couldn't prove anything. And perhaps most significantly, anyone attempting to disprove the existence of laws of logic would have to first assume that laws of logic do exist in order to make the argument. He would refute himself.

When a claim must be accepted as true in order to argue against it, it would be absurd to deny the truth of that claim. Therefore, any debate over fundamental necessities of knowledge (such as laws of logic) will necessarily use some degree of circular reasoning. Such reasoning is not fallacious, providing the claim in question has justification after the fact, and providing the circle is self-consistent. Only inconsistent or arbitrary circles of knowledge involving such fundamental truths should be considered fallacious. This line of reasoning turns out to be the most powerful argument for the biblical worldview, since all non-biblical circles of knowledge are ultimately arbitrary and inconsistent.

However, circular reasoning is fallacious if it is used in arguments that do not involve necessary foundational truth claims. And it is these kinds of arguments that are quite frequent in origins debates. So most of the examples of circular reasoning used by evolutionists are of the fallacious begging-the-question variety — they are arbitrary. In my experience, most evolutionists are not aware that they are begging the question; they seem to have tremendous difficulty thinking in terms of the creation worldview, even as a hypothetical. Consider the evolutionist who argues, "The Bible cannot be correct because it says that stars were created in a single day; but we now know that it takes millions of years for stars to form." By assuming that stars form over millions of years, the critic has taken for granted that they were not supernaturally created. He has tacitly assumed the Bible is wrong in his attempt to argue that the Bible is wrong; he has begged the question.

Another example is, "We know evolution must have happened, because we are here!" This argument begs the question, since the *way* we got here is the very point in question.

Induction and Begging the Question

I want to address a particular instance of begging the question that is extremely common in origins debates, and yet often very difficult to spot for those unfamiliar with the topic. It concerns the nature of a principle of reasoning and science called "induction." *Induction* is the principle of drawing a general inference from many specific instances. In particular, induction is the principle we use when we rely upon past experience as a good indicator of what is likely to happen in the future. For example, every time I have burned my hand on a candle in the past, it has hurt. Therefore, I assume (on the basis of induction) that in the future if I burn my hand on a candle, it will again hurt.

I have pointed out in personal conversations and debates with evolutionists that induction is actually a biblical creationist principle. Namely, it is because God has promised to uphold the future in a way consistent with the past (e.g., Gen. 8:22) that I have a good reason to believe that the future will be like the past, in terms of general principles. This, of course, does not mean that conditions in the future will be exactly like they have been in the past, but the general cycles and principles of nature (i.e., the laws of nature) will be in the future as they have been in the past. Thus, I can use past experience as an indicator of what will probably happen in the future, if I know the conditions sufficiently well. However, evolutionists have no reason in principle (on their own worldview) for believing in induction, yet they all do. They are tacitly relying

28

upon a biblical principle, all the while denying the Bible with their lips — an inconsistency.

In responding to this, evolutionists have attempted to argue that they do indeed have a reason for believing in induction. And that reason is — it works! Every time we have used induction in our personal or scientific endeavors, it has proven to be successful. This gives us confidence (they say) that it will continue to be successful in the future. But in making this argument, the evolutionist has begged the question. His argument is essentially this: "Induction has worked well in the past. Therefore, it will probably work well in the future, too." Of course, this argument assumes that past experience is indicative of what will probably happen in the future. In other words, it assumes the principle of induction. But that is the very question being asked! The evolutionist has arbitrarily assumed the principle of induction in making an argument for the principle of induction. He is reasoning in a circle.

In their textbook on logic, Copi and Cohen state it this way:

> Powerful minds sometimes are snared by this fallacy. . . . Logicians have long sought to establish the reliability of inductive procedures by establishing the truth of what is called the "principle of induction." This is the principle that the laws of nature will operate tomorrow as they operate today, that in basic ways nature is essentially uniform, and that therefore we may rely on past experience to guide our conduct in the future. "That the future will be essentially like the past" is the claim at issue, but this claim, never doubted in ordinary life, turns out to be very difficult to prove. Some thinkers have claimed that they could prove it by showing that, when we have in the past relied on the inductive principle, we have always found that this method has helped to achieve our objectives. They ask, "Why conclude that the future will be like the past?" and answer, "Because it always has been like the past."
>
> But as David Hume pointed out, this common argument is a *petitio*, it begs the question. For the point at issue is whether

nature will continue to behave regularly; that it has done so in the past cannot serve as proof that it will do so in the future — unless one assumes the very principle that is here in question: that the future will be like the past.[3]

Conclusions

Watch for arguments that subtly presume (in an arbitrary way) what the critic is attempting to prove. In particular, evolutionists will often take for granted the assumptions of naturalism, uniformitarianism, strict empiricism (the notion that all truth claims are answered by observation and experimentation), and sometimes evolution itself. But, of course, these are the very claims at issue. When an evolutionist takes these things for granted, he is not giving a good logical reason for his position; he is simply arbitrarily asserting his position.

Examples of Begging the Question

"Evolution must be true. After all, it is a well-established fact of science."

"We have confidence in the methods of science and induction because they have served us so well in the past."

"How do we know that laws of physics are universal? Because everywhere on earth we've tested them, they work quite well. So it is reasonable to assume they are the same elsewhere."

"Creation cannot be true because it involves the supernatural."

"The Bible must be true because it says it is the Word of God, and God would not lie."

"The Koran must be true because it says it is the Word of God, and God would not lie."

"We don't actually need evidence for evolution, because it is a fact."

a baseless unsupported assertion masqurading as true fact

Endnotes

1. The parting of the Red Sea was certainly a miracle — an extraordinary act of God (Exod. 14:21). Yet God used wind — a force of nature — to accomplish this miracle.

2. It is always necessary to presuppose the *preconditions of intelligibility*. These are foundation truth claims necessary for reasoning and include such things as laws of logic, the basic reliability of sense experience, and induction. These things make sense in light of Scripture, even though we must use them in arguing for them. Thus, the Christian can justify them after the fact. However, the evolutionist assumes these arbitrarily — without rational justification — and has thus begged the question.

3. I.M. Copi and C. Cohen, *Introduction to Logic* tenth edition (Upper Saddle River, NJ: Prentice Hall, 1998), p. 187.

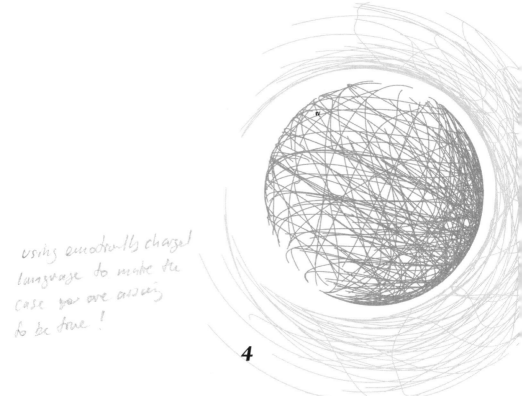

using emotionally charged language to make the case you are assuming to be true!

4

Question-begging Epithet

a discriptive word (nickname) used or added to substitued for a person name.

One of the most common fallacies committed by evolutionists on the Internet is the fallacy of the question-begging epithet. This could be considered a specific sub-type of begging the question (the fallacy of merely assuming what one is trying to prove).

With the question-begging epithet, the arguer uses biased (often emotional) language to persuade people rather than using logic. For example, if a reporter said, "This criminal is charged with violently murdering the innocent victim," she would be using a question-begging epithet because she has used biased language to make a case that is not yet logically established. It would have been more objective for her to say, "This suspect is charged with killing the other person."

emotionally charged words

Some great examples of question-begging epithets can be found on some evolution Internet sites — particularly forums or blogs. I saw one example where an evolutionist wrote, "Our department is becoming <u>infested</u> with creationists." The word *infested* is emotionally charged and portrays creationists in a bad light without making any argument for this. Another writer stated, "To be a creationist, you'd have to ignore tons of scientific evidence." This remark is the fallacy of the question-begging epithet because it uses biased language (and not logic) to suggest that scientific evidence supports evolution.

There is a place for emotional language. After all, language has other purposes than to make logical arguments. It can be used to inform, to question, to command, and to evoke. However, when people try to evoke an emotional response to persuade others of a point that is logically questionable, the fallacy of the question-begging epithet is committed.

Yelling or vulgar language during a debate is always an example of this fallacy. Many times people will turn up the vocal volume to compensate for a lack of cogency in their argument. Ironically, many of those who use mocking or vulgar language in forums seem to think that their rhetoric constitutes a good argument (as in the illustration). Far from it. Such language is an indication of a serious lack of critical thinking skills.[1]

Question-begging epithets can be subtle. Consider this phrase: "Evolution vs. creationism." By attaching -*ism* to the end of creation but not to evolution, the person is subtly suggesting that creation is merely a belief, whereas evolution is not. But he or she has made no argument for this.

"Creationists believe that the universe is young, but the best scientists tell us that it is billions of years old." By using the adjective "best" to describe those scientists who believe in an old universe, this argument uses biased language rather than logic to persuade. It is fallacious.

Here is another example: "The Creation 'Museum' isn't about science at all, but is entirely about a peculiar, quirky, very specific interpretation of the Bible." The author provided no support for this opinion; it is simply an emotional reaction. He also attempts to deride the Creation Museum by putting the word *museum* in quotes. His claim is nothing but a fallacious epithet. When people use sarcastic/sardonic statements in place of logic, they commit the fallacy of the question-begging epithet. For example, "Yeah, Tyrannosauridae were herbovirus [sic] too before The Fall [sic]. With razor sharp teeth to kill the tenacious shrubberies!" Such statements are designed to stir people's emotions, thereby distracting them from the realization that no logical case has been made.

> **Question-begging epithet**
>
> —
>
> *using biased (often emotional) language to persuade people rather than using logic*

Another common example is when someone accuses an opponent of committing a logical fallacy when it is not the case. A false accusation of a logical fallacy is itself a logical fallacy. This might happen, for example, after a creationist has politely and cogently pointed out a number of fallacies in an evolutionist's reasoning, and then makes a good argument for creation. In an attempt to turn the tables, the evolutionist responds by saying, "Well, that's a fallacy!" But he has made no logical case that the creationist has indeed committed a fallacy, which makes the evolutionist's claim itself an arbitrary question-begging epithet.

In Ephesians 5:6 we read, "Let no one deceive you with empty words, for because of these things the wrath of God comes upon the sons of disobedience." An evolutionist may be very emotionally committed to his position and may use biased (or mocking) language in an attempt to evoke a similar emotion in others. However, this is logically irrelevant to whether or not his belief is true.

When people use mere rhetoric ("empty words") without providing a logical reason for their position, we must cordially point out that they have not made a logical argument; they are simply being arbitrary. Conversely, Christians are to take the "high ground" and always give a good reason for the confidence within us (1 Pet. 3:15).

Examples of the Question-begging Epithet

"Evolution vs. creationism."

"Creation vs. science."

"Creation is so obviously wrong that I don't need to even argue my position!"

[vulgar language]

"The scientific position is evolution. Creation is just religious nonsense."

"God is arguably the most unpleasant character in all of fiction."

"Why do I not believe in creation? Because I'm intelligent."

"I used to have blind faith just like you, but then I 'evolved.' "

Endnotes

1. There are several evolution blogs that consist of virtually nothing but emotionally charged language. The authors make no logical case for their position, and students of logic will easily recognize that such rhetoric is nothing more than emotional venting (much like a child throwing a tantrum). I encourage readers to check out some popular evolution blogs/forums to see examples of this. However, be warned that many of these sites contain vulgar language and/or images. This itself is an indication of the intellectual bankruptcy of the evolutionary position; since evolutionists have no cogent arguments for their view, they must resort to such emotionalism.

Loaded = slanted / biased in their favour

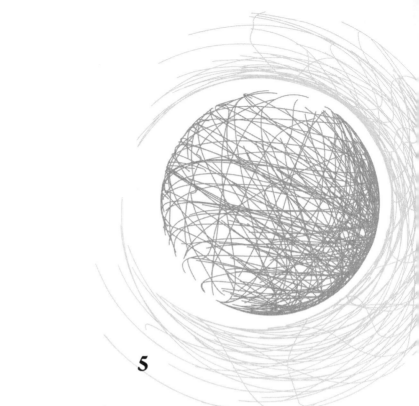

5

Complex Question

Similar to the question-begging epithet is the fallacy called *complex question*. This is the interrogative form of begging the question — when the arguer attempts to persuade by asking a loaded question. A classic example is this: "Have you stopped beating your wife?" Either a yes or no answer would seem to imply that the person did in the past beat his wife, which may not be the case. The question is "complex" because it should be divided into two questions:

1. Did you ever beat your wife?
2. If so, have you now stopped doing this?

Here are some common evolutionary examples of the fallacy of complex question: "Why are creationists against science?" This loaded question presumes that creationists are against science, which is not the case. It should have been divided:

1. Are creationists against science?
2. If so, why?

Since the answer to the first is no, the second question is not necessary.

"Why is evolution so critical to our understanding of biology?" is fallacious because we should first ask, "Is evolution critical to our understanding of biology?" Watch for loaded questions in evolutionary literature such as, "How were dinosaurs able to survive for millions of years?" This is the fallacy of the complex question because it should be divided:

1. Did dinosaurs indeed survive for millions of years?
2. If so, how?

> **Complex question**
>
> —
>
> *attempting to persuade by asking a loaded question*

"What is the mechanism by which reptiles evolved into birds?" "If the earth truly is 6,000 years old as you creationists say, then why do we find rocks that are over four billion years old?" "If creation is true, then why does all the scientific evidence point to evolution?" These are all fallacious arguments that use loaded questions to persuade rather than logic.

One time, after I gave a presentation on creation, an atheist came up to me and asked, "Are you aware of the fact that . . . ?" Before he could complete the sentence, I strongly suspected that it was going to be the fallacy of the complex question. Sure enough, what he was rhetorically asserting to be a fact was not true at all. He had misunderstood some of the things I had presented and had committed some errors in reasoning as well. People sometimes use the formula "Are you aware of the fact that X?" to persuade others of X, when in fact X is logically unproved.

Persuasion by rhetorical trickery rather than logic

Replace logic with deceitful trickery. Conclusion via conning

What people judge to be a fallacy often depends on their worldview. Consider this question: "Have you repented of your sins?"

A non-Christian may consider this to be a complex question and would want it divided:

1. Have you ever sinned?
2. If so, have you repented?

From a Christian worldview, however, the question is not complex because we know that all have sinned (Rom. 3:23).

Along with the question-begging epithet, the complex question uses biased language in place of logical argumentation. When the evolutionists commit either of these fallacies, we must gently point out that they have not actually made a logical argument. They have rhetorically assumed what they are trying to prove and have, thus, begged the very question at issue.

Examples of the Complex Question

"If creation is true, then why does all the evidence point to evolution?"

"If the world is young, then why does it look so old?"

"Why are creationists against science?"

"Are you aware of the fact that evolution has been demonstrated in a laboratory?"

"How did life arise from random chemicals and diversify into all the species we see on earth today?"

"How is it that scientists are able to probe the distant past, and learn what life was like millions of years ago?"

"When are you going to stop believing nonsense and accept science?"

Break de question down

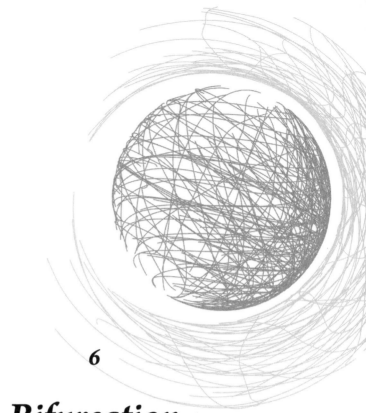

6

Bifurcation

Aperson commits the fallacy of bifurcation when he or she claims that there are only two mutually exclusive possibilities — when, in fact, there is a third option (or more). For this reason the fallacy is also known as the *either-or fallacy* and the *false dilemma*.

A facetious example is this: "Either the traffic light is red or it is green." This is obviously fallacious, since the light could be yellow.[1]

A more realistic example is this: "Either you have faith or you are rational." This commits the fallacy of bifurcation, since there is a third possibility: we can have faith and be rational. In fact, faith is essential in order to have rationality (e.g., to make sense of laws of logic).[2]

"Either the universe operates in a law-like fashion, or God is constantly performing miracles." This is also fallacious because a third

> ### *Bifurcation*
> —
> *claiming there are only two mutually exclusive possibilities, when there may actually be three or more options*

possibility exists: the universe operates in a law-like fashion most of the time, and God occasionally performs miracles.

Sometimes the origins debate is framed as "faith vs. reason," "science or religion," or the "Bible vs. science." These are all false dilemmas. Faith and reason are not contrary. They go well together (since all reasoning presupposes a type of faith).[3]

Likewise, science and religion (the Christian religion, to be specific) are not mutually exclusive. In fact, it is the Christian system that makes sense of science and the uniformity of nature. Likewise, the debate should never be framed as "the Bible vs. science," since the procedures of science are fully compatible with the Bible. In fact, science is based on the biblical worldview; science requires predictability in nature, which is only made possible by the fact that God upholds the universe in a consistent way that is congenial to human understanding. Such predictability just wouldn't make sense in a "chance" universe.

The fallacy of bifurcation may be more difficult to spot when the person merely implies that only two options exist, rather than explicitly stating this.

"I could never live by faith because I am a rational person." This sentence tacitly presents us with only two options: either faith or rationality. But, as we've mentioned before, these are not exclusive. A rational person must have some degree of faith. So, the Christian takes the third, unmentioned option: faith *and* rationality.[4] "The Bible teaches that 'in Christ all things hold together' (Col. 1:17). But we now know that the forces of gravity and electromagnetism are what hold the universe together." This is an example of the fallacy of bifurcation because the critic has implicitly assumed that either (1) God holds the universe together, or (2) gravity and electromagnetism do. However, these are not exclusive. "Gravity" and "electromagnetism" are simply the names we give to the way in which God holds the universe together. Laws of nature are not a replacement for God's power. Rather, they are an *example* of God's power.[5]

"You must not really believe that God is going to answer your request for healing; otherwise you would not have gone to the doctor." The implicit false dilemma here is that either the doctor will help the person or God will. But why can't it be both? God can use human actions as part of the means by which He accomplishes His will.

On the other hand, in some situations there really are only two options; and it is not fallacious to say so. "Either my car is in the garage, or it is not the case that my car is in the garage" commits no fallacy.[6] When Jesus states, "He who is not with Me is against Me" (Matt. 12:30), He has not committed any fallacy because God is in a position to tell us that there is no third ("neutral") option. (An attempt to be neutral toward God is sinful and, therefore, non-neutral.)[7] The key to spotting fallacies of bifurcation is to watch for cases when only two options are presented (either explicitly or implicitly) and to consider carefully whether or not there is a third possibility.

Examples of Bifurcation

"Either evolution is true, or everything we know about the world is wrong."

"Either you have reasons for what you believe, or you simply take it on faith."

"I could never be a creationist, because I'm rational." [either creation or rationality]

"Well, do you believe the universe is governed by natural laws, or do you believe it is upheld by the hand of God?"

"I listen to the Holy Spirit to tell me what to do, not the text of the Bible." ["either the Holy Spirit *or* the Bible" when it should be "the Holy Spirit *by* the Bible."]

"Does God determine our actions, or do we have freedom of choice?"

Endnotes

1. In logic, red and green are said to be contrary, but not contradictory options. When two propositions are contradictory, one of them is true, and the other is false. A proposition can be turned into its contradiction by adding, "It is not the case that. . . ." So the statements "the light is red" and "it is not the case that the light is red" are contradictory. However, when two propositions are contrary, they can both be false, but they cannot both be true.

2. For the demonstration of this, see Jason Lisle, *The Ultimate Proof of Creation* (Green Forest, AR: Master Books, 2009).

3. Faith is belief in what has not been observed by the senses (see Heb. 11:1). In order to reason logically, a person must believe in laws of logic. However, laws of logic are immaterial and therefore cannot be observed by the senses. So belief in laws of logic is a type of faith. Moreover, laws of logic have rational justification only in the Christian faith system.

4. To be specific, it is "rationality *because* of faith." It is the Christian faith that makes rationality possible.

5. Otherwise, there would be no reason to think that the laws of nature apply universally or that they will apply in the future as they have in the past. Only the consistent Christian has rational justification for such uniformity in nature.

6. There can be no third option when the two options are X and not-X. This is the law of the excluded middle.

7. Our thinking is to be in submission to Christ (2 Cor. 10:5). When the critic attempts to be "neutral," he is refusing to submit his thinking to Christ. The critic's position is rebellious and, therefore, non-neutral.

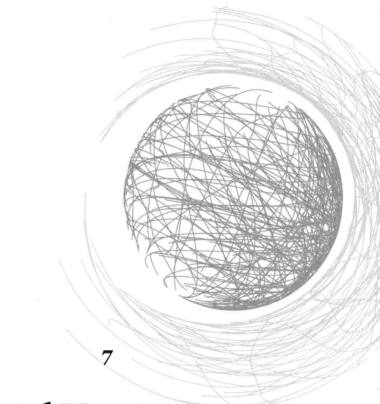

7

Ad Hominem

The phrase *ad hominem* is Latin and means "to the man." The fallacy is so named because it directs an argument against the *person* making a claim rather than the claim itself. The critic hopes that people will reject his opponent's claim simply on the basis that there is something objectionable about the person making the claim. For example, "You cannot honestly accept John's claims about politics because he can't even find a job!" However, John's inability to find employment is logically irrelevant to the political claim he is making.

The fallacy comes in two varieties: abusive *ad hominem* and circumstantial *ad hominem*. In the abusive *ad hominem,* the critic attacks his opponent's character or insults him in an attempt to discredit him in the eyes of the audience. This tactic is common in politics, and it may

discredit

psychologically sway people. However, it is *logically* fallacious because a person's character (or lack thereof) is logically irrelevant to the validity of his argument. Even if the critic's negative claims about his opponent are true (e.g., he really is a draft-dodger, or he really did spend time in jail), this has no bearing on the position he is advocating.

Name-calling is perhaps the most obvious form of the abusive *ad hominem* fallacy. When children have a heated disagreement, they sometimes engage in such behavior. As we grow up, we are supposed to become rational and learn to make arguments based on logical reasoning. However, since there is no rationally sound argument for evolution, evolutionists are increasingly resorting to name-calling. I recall a particular instance where an evolutionist launched into a name-calling diatribe against Ken Ham.[1] Such immature behavior reminds us that the evolutionary worldview is utterly intellectually bankrupt.[2]

> *Ad hominem*
> —
> *directing an argument against the person making the claim rather than the claim itself*

The circumstantial *ad hominem* fallacy is when a critic simply dismisses a person's argument based on the arguer's circumstances. Suppose Susie makes an argument that taxes on gasoline should be increased. Her opponent, Bobby, tries to refute this by pointing out that Susie's job is tax-supported, so she is strongly motivated to argue for higher taxes. Bobby concludes that Susie's argument is wrong since Susie has a bias. Bobby has committed the circumstantial *ad hominem* fallacy — just because Susie is strongly motivated to defend a particular position does not mean that her argument is faulty.

A non-Christian might argue: "Christianity isn't true. You just believe in Christianity because you were brought up in a Christian home. If you were brought up in the Islamic religion, you would be a Muslim now."

This is the circumstantial *ad hominem* fallacy because the circumstances by which the person became a Christian are not relevant to his or her argument for Christianity. While it may be true that I am much

48

more likely to become a Christian by virtue of being reared in a Christian home, this is utterly irrelevant to whether or not I have a really good logical argument for Christianity. It would be just like saying, "You just believe in the multiplication table because you were taught it in school!" It is true that I probably would not have discovered the multiplication table without someone teaching it to me, but this does not mean that I don't have some really good reasons to continue to believe in the multiplication table!

An evolutionist might argue: "Creation isn't true. You just believe in creation because you read that stuff on the Answers in Genesis website!"

Although the information on the website may have helped people to see the truth of creation and how to argue for it (we hope so!), the person's argument should be evaluated on its own merit, not on how he arrived at it. The evolutionist is wrong to simply dismiss an argument because he doesn't like the source.[3] The source is not relevant to the argument's validity.

It may help to note that there is often a difference between a *cause* and a *reason*. What is the *cause* of a person believing in the Christian worldview? Many factors may have contributed: conversations with family, a sermon, prayers of friends, and ultimately the Holy Spirit (1 Cor. 12:3).

What is the *reason* (i.e., the rational justification) for a person believing in the Christian worldview? One really good reason would be that Christianity alone can account for laws of logic,[4] and science.[5] In the above examples, the critic is arbitrarily dismissing a *reason* for a position on the basis that he does not like the *cause* of the person coming to that position. But such a dismissal is logically unwarranted and fallacious.

Not all references to a person's character are necessarily *ad hominem* fallacies. For example, if a person makes a particular assertion (not an *argument*, but merely an *assertion*), and if it can be demonstrated that the person is generally dishonest, it would be perfectly appropriate and relevant to point out that his dishonesty calls into question his credibility on the claim.[6] However, even this does not *disprove* the person's assertion, since a generally dishonest person will sometimes tell the truth. Moreover, if the person makes an *argument*, his or her alleged dishonesty is totally irrelevant to the validity of that argument. (An argument is not the same as an assertion.)[7] The key is to remember that an argument should be based on its merit, not on the alleged character defects or the circumstances of the person making the argument.

Example of *Ad Hominem*

"If you don't believe in evolution, then you're pretty much just a moron!"

"Creationists are really uneducated; you shouldn't bother listening to their arguments."

"The reason you believe in creation is because you were raised in a Christian home."

"The folks at Answers in Genesis argue for creation because if they didn't they would be fired."

"You simply believe in God as an intellectual crutch. You cannot stand the thought of being alone in the universe, so you invent an imaginary friend."

[any pejorative language directed at a person without logical support]

"Well, of course you believe in creation. You work at a Christian school."

Endnotes

1. See "Evolving Tactics," www.answersingenesis.org/articles/am/v4/n1/evolving-tactics.
2. Evolution cannot account for rationality, morality, or the success of science, as documented in *The Ultimate Proof of Creation*.
3. Phrased this way, such a mistake in reasoning is called the *genetic fallacy* (see chapter 11). *Ad hominem* fallacies can be considered a *type* of the genetic fallacy.
4. See "Atheism: An Irrational Worldview," www.answersingenesis.org/articles/aid/v2/n1/atheism-irrational.

5. See "Evolution: The Anti-science," www.answersingenesis.org/articles/aid/v3/n1/evolution-anti-science.

6. However, people cannot rationally assert that their opponent is lying on the basis that they disagree on the very claim at issue — that would be begging the question. As an example, consider the evolutionist who says, "Creationists are liars because they teach that the universe is only thousands of years old and that the first life on earth was supernaturally created." The evolutionist's assertion is only true if evolution is, but that is the very claim at issue. So the evolutionist has simply begged the question.

7. An assertion is a proposition, whereas an argument is a chain of propositions where the truth of one is claimed to follow from the others. Logical fallacies concern the "chain of reasoning" between propositions, not the truthfulness of the propositions themselves. See the introduction chapter for a review of these distinctions.

artificial authors

8

Faulty Appeal to Authority

T he faulty appeal to authority is, in a way, the opposite of the *ad hominem* fallacy. Whereas the *ad hominem* fallacy denies a claim based on the person making it, the faulty appeal to authority endorses a claim simply based on the person making it. Essentially, the faulty appeal to authority is the argument that a claim is true simply because someone else believes it.

The basic structure of the argument is this:

1. Bill believes X.
2. Therefore, X is true.

Of course, it is almost never stated this explicitly. Often the person to whom the appeal is made is considered highly esteemed for one reason or

> **Faulty appeal to authority**
>
> —
>
> *endorsing a claim simply based on the person making it*

another. But the truthfulness of the claim at issue is not necessarily relevant to the popularity of the individual making the claim.

In the origins debate, the faulty appeal is often to someone who is considered an expert on a particular topic — a scientist or perhaps a theologian. For example, consider the statement, "Dr. Bill has a Ph.D. in biology, and he believes in evolution." The unstated conclusion is that evolution must therefore be true or is at least likely to be true. But such an argument is fallacious. After all, we could equally point out that "Dr. Dave also has a Ph.D. in biology, and he believes in *biblical creation*." The fact that other experts on the topic draw the opposite conclusion should reveal the vacuous nature of the evolutionist's argument.

Another example would be this: "Jim has a doctorate in theology, and he says it's okay to believe in evolution and the Bible."

Again, we could certainly find many qualified theologians who would state the exact opposite. While it is okay to consider what a theologian has to say about the Bible, it is infinitely more important to consider what the Bible actually states!

If an expert on U.S. law claimed that the Constitution does not contain the phrase "We the people," would that make it so? We could easily refute his claim by simply reading from an actual copy of the Constitution. The fact that he is an expert does not override the evidence.

Not all appeals to authority are *faulty* appeals to authority. It is legitimate to consider the opinion of an expert on a particular topic. None of us has the time or the ability to verify each and every truth claim that has ever been made. We can and should rely upon the expertise of others at times. So when does the appeal to authority become a fallacy? It seems there are three common ways in which this occurs:

1. **Appealing to an expert in an area that is not his area of expertise.** Our hypothetical Dr. Bill may indeed have a Ph.D. in biology — and that qualifies him to say something

about how organisms function today. But does knowledge of how things work today necessarily imply knowledge of how things came to be? This is a separate question. The experiments Dr. Bill has done and the observations he has made have all taken place in the present world. He has no more direct observations of the ancient past than anyone else today.[1] The question of origins is a history question that deals with worldviews. It is not really a biology question, and so, Dr. Bill's opinion on the topic of origins isn't necessarily any more qualified than any other opinion.

2. **Failure to consider the worldview of the expert and how this might affect his interpretation of the data.** We all have a world-and-life view — a philosophy that guides our understanding of the universe. When we interpret scientific and historical evidence, we use this philosophy to draw conclusions.[2] The fact that Dr. Bill believes in evolution means that he is predisposed to interpret the evidence in a particular way. (My point is not to fault him for this; everyone has biases. Rather, we should simply be mindful of what his biases are.) A creationist with the same credentials might draw a very different conclusion from the same data. So while I may put confidence in what Dr. Bill says about the structure of a particular protein that he has studied under the microscope, I would not put much confidence in his opinions on question of origins since his bias in that area is faulty.

3. **Treating a fallible expert as infallible.** We should also keep in mind that even experts do not know everything. They can make mistakes even in their own field. Some new discovery may cause a scientist to change his mind about something that he thought he knew. So at best, appealing to an expert yields only a probable conclusion. It would be fallacious to argue that something definitely must be true simply because a (fallible) expert believes it.

Of course, if the expert had knowledge of everything and never lied, then there would be no fallacy in accepting his statements as absolutely true. In fact, it would be absurd to not do so under those circumstances. The Bible claims to be such an infallible source — a revelation from the God who knows everything and cannot lie (Col. 2:3; Titus 1:2). Thus, there is no fallacy in appealing to Scripture as absolutely authoritative. Some evolutionists have mistakenly accused creationists of committing the faulty appeal to authority on this very issue. Granted, the evolutionist may not believe that the Bible is an infallible source, but he would have to demonstrate this before accusing the creationist of a faulty appeal.

Another type of faulty appeal to authority is the appeal to the majority. This is when a person argues that a claim must be true simply because most people believe it. But, of course, just because a majority of people believe something does not make it so. History is replete with examples of when the majority was totally wrong. Truth is not decided by a vote, after all.

This fallacy is so obvious it is hard to believe that people would fall for it. But there is something very psychologically seductive about the appeal to the majority. We are inclined to think, "How could all those people be wrong?"[3] Of course, it could well be the case that many people in that majority are convinced of the claim at issue for exactly the same reason: because all the *other* people in that majority believe it (which is no *logical* reason at all).

The appeal to the majority is often combined with the appeal to an expert — an appeal to the majority of experts. Evolutionists often commit this double fallacy; they try to support their case by pointing out: "The vast majority of scientists believe in evolution. Therefore, evolution is very likely to be true."

However, simply adding two fallacies together does not form a good argument! Again, we could point to many historical examples of cases where the scientific consensus was dead wrong. Yet, people continue to perpetuate this fallacy.

We sometimes hear phrases like "according to mainstream science . . . ," "the scientific establishment . . . ," or "the scientific consensus is . . ." as alleged proof of a particular claim.

Another example is this: "Creationists teach that the world is roughly 6,000 years old, but the majority of scientists disagree." This sentence is true, but the unstated conclusion is that we must accept the opinion of the majority of experts — which is logically fallacious. As with a single expert, it is not fallacious to consider the opinion of a group of experts. However, as before, we should consider whether they are qualified in the issue under investigation, be mindful of their worldview and biases, and keep in mind that they are fallible people with finite knowledge.

I believe that God gave people different interests and is pleased when they study hard and develop expertise on some aspect of His creation. It is commendable to esteem the opinion of experts, provided that we are discerning and never regard fallible human opinions above (or equal to) the authoritative Word of God.

Examples of the Faulty Appeal to Authority

"If creation is true, then why do the vast majority of scientists believe in evolution?"

"Of course evolution is true. My biology textbook says so."

"Dr. So-and-so believes in evolution. So clearly it is true."

"The scientific consensus is that the world is billions of years old." [implying "therefore we should believe it"]

"Of course all life evolved from a common ancestor. How could all those scientists be wrong?"

"You trust what the scientists say about gravity, electricity, chemistry, etc. Why do you doubt what they say about evolution?"

"Jim is one of the smartest people I know. And he believes in evolution." [implication: "Therefore, we should too."]

Appeal to authority but the logic of the argument— distinct from that!

Endnotes

1. For some reason, it is common for people to think that paleontologists and geologists study the past. But this is not so. Rocks and fossils exist in the present (otherwise we wouldn't have access to them). Although there is nothing wrong with speculating about past events (e.g., how fossils or rocks formed) and then testing the plausibility of such models with experiments in the present, we should keep in mind that the past is never actually observable or open to scientific investigation.

2. Some evolutionists might claim that they have no philosophy — that our interpretations of evidence should be "neutral" and unbiased. But this is a philosophy in and of itself, albeit a very bad one since it is self-refuting.

3. *Sin* is the answer to this question. All people have a sin nature. Those who have not had their minds regenerated by the Holy Spirit are not capable of drawing correct conclusions on spiritual matters (1 Cor. 2:14). The unbeliever is not a neutral, objective observer. He is rebellious and strongly motivated to reject the biblical God (Rom. 1:18–20).

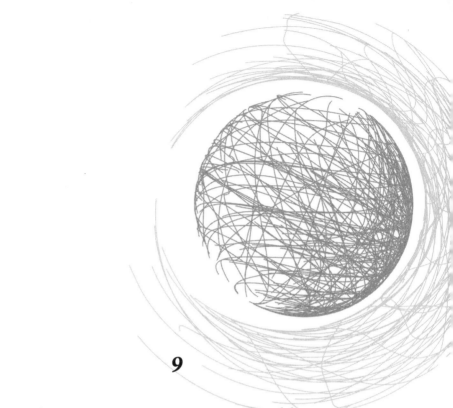

9

The Strawman Fallacy

It's a fallacy that just shouldn't happen — but it does all the time. The straw-man fallacy is when a person misrepresents his opponent's position and then proceeds to refute that misrepresentation (i.e., the "straw man") rather than what his opponent actually claims.[1] Sometimes evolutionists will say or imply something along these lines: "Creationists do not believe that animals change. But clearly, animals do change. So creationists are mistaken."

Since creationists do indeed believe that animals change (just not from one basic created kind to another), the argument is a straw-man fallacy. The argument does not refute what creationists *actually* claim.

Such a misrepresentation could be unintentional; it could be that a particular evolutionist simply misunderstands what a creationist is teaching. Or the fallacy could be quite deliberate. That, of course, is a dishonest approach, yet it is quite common in origins debates.

Even in cases where the misrepresentation is unintentional, there is still a degree of liability. After all, the arguer should have done sufficient research and studied what the opponent actually teaches. We would certainly be willing to overlook minor misunderstandings, particularly where a position is complex or nuanced (though the critic should still be corrected on the issue). However, there are a number of cases where the creationist position is so clear that misrepresentations by evolutionists are simply inexcusable. The following are a few examples.

If an evolutionist were to claim, "Creationists don't believe in science," this would be a strawman fallacy.[2] Creationists do believe in science. There are several full-time Ph.D. scientists on the Answers in Genesis staff. I've argued openly that biblical creation is what makes science possible.

Someone may claim, "Creationists believe in the fixity of species." However, this is certainly not the mainstream biblical creationist position. There may be a few individuals who hold to such a concept, but it is not the position advocated by most creationists. Thus, the generalization "creationists believe . . ." is false.

Likewise, the claim "Creationists say there are no good mutations" is not representative of what biblical creationists teach. Generally, we say that mutations do not add brand-new, creative information to the genome and are thus in the "wrong direction" to make evolution happen. But we do believe that mutations can result in traits that increase survival value under certain conditions.

The statement "Answers in Genesis is pushing to get creation taught in public schools alongside evolution" is definitely false. Answers in Genesis as a ministry is not about political or legal change. Rather, we are about defending the Bible from the very first verse and teaching other Christians to do the same. Our desire is to equip Christians. It is the Church we would like to see change. Of course, as more Christians learn to defend their faith well, this may eventually result in a changed political and legal situation. However, we do not (as a ministry) attempt to change laws or get involved in politics. And we have stated that as a ministry we are against mandating that creation be taught in public schools.

> *The strawman fallacy*
> —
> *misrepresenting an opponent's position and proceeding to refute the misrepresentation rather than what the opponent actually claims*

"The Bible teaches that the earth has literal pillars and corners and cannot be moved. It is clearly wrong." This is a misrepresentation of Scripture and therefore constitutes a straw-man fallacy. The Bible uses figures of speech (just as we do when we say, "Tim is a pillar of the community") and poetic language at times. Referring to the cardinal directions as "corners" (Isa. 11:12)[3] or the stability of the earth as not able to "be moved" (Ps. 93:1)[4] is not an error. It is entirely inappropriate for a critic to take the poetic sections of the Bible as literal — or the literal historical sections as poetic. Many objections against Scripture turn out to be straw-man fallacies.

The claims that creationists believe in a flat earth, that we deny laws of nature, or that we take every verse of the Bible in a wooden literal sense are all baseless assertions. Nonetheless, claiming that creationists believe in such things makes the creation position easier to discredit — but it is not a rationally cogent way to debate. Granted, not all evolutionists do this; some do accurately represent their opponents. But ignorance of biblical creation among those who oppose it is a serious problem — one that Christian apologists must be prepared to face.

We must gently encourage our opponents to find out what it is that creationists actually teach. This is not a difficult task. Our positions on the most-asked questions are well-summarized in *The New Answers Book* series and to a great extent on the *free* Answers in Genesis website (answersingenesis.org).

Creationists must also stay educated on both sides of the issue so that we do not commit the very same fallacy.[5] Watch for misrepresentations of creation or other Christian teachings and be ready to point out that such straw-man arguments are fallacious; yet always do so with gentleness and respect.

Examples of the Strawman Fallacy

"Those folks at Answers in Genesis say that you have to believe in six days of creation in order to be saved."

"Creationists don't believe in the scientific method. They say you should just look to the Bible for all your answers."

"Creationists don't believe in rationality. They take things on blind faith instead."

"The young-earth creationists believe in a worldwide flood, but where did all the water come from? Presumably they believe that all the mountains we see today were eroded down by the Flood, and then built back up again afterward."

"The creationists teach that God created all the species we see on earth as they are now and in their current locations. But scientists have discovered that species have diversified and lived in different locations in the past."

Endnotes

1. The straw-man fallacy is a specific type of the fallacy of irrelevant thesis (see chapter 11). The latter is the fallacy of proving a point that is not at issue. In the case of the straw-man fallacy, proving that the misrepresentation of the opponent's position is false is irrelevant to whether or not his actual position is true or false.

2. It could also be an example of equivocation if the evolutionist conflates operational science with origins science or science with evolution.

3. The Hebrew word translated "corners" indicates an extremity, as in the farthest reaches of the earth. The four extremes would be north, south, east, and west. The Revelation 7:1 passage uses the same type of wording as Isaiah (11:12) to indicate the same cardinal directions. Revelation often alludes to Old Testament imagery.

4. The fact that this occurs in the Psalms is essentially a "giveaway" that it is a poetic passage. The Psalmist uses the same Hebrew word when he says, "I shall not be shaken" (Ps. 62:6), indicating that he will not deviate from the path God created for him.

5. This does happen from time to time, though it isn't nearly as common as the reverse, perhaps because our culture is so saturated with the notion of particles-to-people evolution. Evolution is taught in virtually all public schools in the United States (and usually biblical creation is not); so most creationists are aware of the evolution position. We should also note that all Christians have at one point been non-Christians; so, we can understand how the unbeliever thinks about things. However, non-Christians have difficulty thinking like Christians (even if they were brought up in the Church) because the crucial issues require the enlightening of the Holy Spirit. Indeed, the unbeliever cannot understand spiritual issues apart from God's power (1 Cor. 2:14).

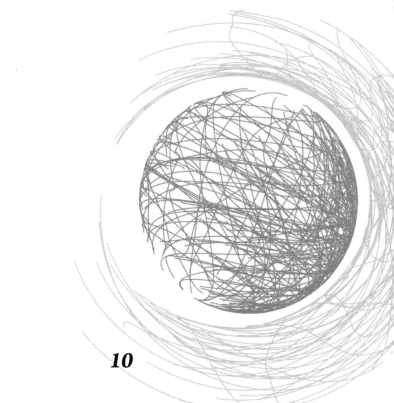

10

Formal Fallacies

I n this chapter we will address two of the most common fallacies that occur in arguments about origins: "affirming the consequent" and "denying the antecedent." Don't be intimidated if you are unfamiliar with these names. They are easier to understand than they appear. These are *formal* fallacies because the mistake in reasoning stems from the structure (the *form*) of the argument. It is well worth the effort to study formal fallacies and their corresponding terminology because these two fallacies are extremely common — perhaps the two most common fallacies committed by evolutionists.

> *Formal fallacies*
> —
> *mistakes in reasoning stemming from the structure (the form) of the argument*

> **Hypothetical proposition**
>
> —
>
> *a proposition stating that if part A is true, then part B must be true as well*

> **Mixed hypothetical syllogism**
>
> —
>
> *an argument with two premises, only one of which is hypothetical*

Formal deductive arguments can be put into a symbolic notation with letters representing the propositions. Consider the proposition, "If it is snowing, then it must be cold outside." This proposition has the basic form: "If p, then q." Any proposition that has that form ("if p, then q") is called a "hypothetical proposition." This is because it's not asserting either p or q; it is merely stating that if p hypothetically were true, then q would have to be true as well. In a hypothetical proposition the first part (p) is called the antecedent, and the second part (q) is called the consequent. In our example, "it is snowing" is the antecedent, and "it must be cold outside" is the consequent.

If an argument has two premises, only one of which is hypothetical, then it is called a "mixed hypothetical syllogism." Here is an example:

1. If it is snowing, then it must be cold outside.
2. It is snowing.
3. Therefore, it is cold outside.

In this argument, the first premise (if p, then q) is hypothetical. The second premise (p) is not hypothetical; it asserts that it is indeed snowing. And the conclusion is q. Since the second premise affirms that p (the antecedent) is true, this type of argument is called "affirming the antecedent" and is perfectly valid. (Recall, "valid" means that if the premises are true, so is the conclusion.) The Latin name for this type of argument is *modus ponens,* which means the "method of affirming."

> **Affirming the consequent**
>
> —
>
> *an argument where the second premise affirms the consequent of the first premise*

66

Affirming the Consequent

There is a fallacy that is very similar to *modus ponens* and has this form:

1. If p, then q.
2. q.
3. Therefore, p.

We can see that this is a fallacy by substituting phrases for p and q.

1. If it is snowing, then it must be cold outside.
2. It is cold outside.
3. Therefore, it must be snowing.

But clearly just because it is cold outside does not necessarily mean that it must be snowing. So, this argument is invalid. Since the second premise affirms that the consequent (q) is true, this fallacy is called "affirming the consequent." Here are some common examples:

1. If evolution were true, we would expect to see similarities in DNA of all organisms on earth.
2. We do see similarities in DNA of all organisms on earth.
3. Therefore, evolution is true.

The evolutionist making such an argument has failed to recognize that creationists would also expect to see similarities in DNA of all organisms, since the original kinds were made by the same Creator.

1. If the big bang is true, then we would expect to see a cosmic microwave background.
2. We do see a cosmic microwave background.
3. Therefore, the big bang must be true.

This big-bang supporter has failed to consider other possible causes for the cosmic microwave background. His argument is an example of the fallacy of affirming the consequent.

Another mixed hypothetical syllogism has the following form:

1. If p, then q.
2. Not q.
3. Therefore, not p.

This is a valid argument as can be seen by substituting the phrases for the symbols.

1. If it is snowing, then it must be cold outside.
2. It is not cold outside.
3. Therefore, it is not snowing.

Since the second premise denies that the consequent (q) is true, this valid argument is called "denying the consequent" or, in Latin, *modus tollens,* which means the "method of denying."

> *Denying the antecedent*
>
> —
>
> *an argument where the second premise denies the antecedent of the first premise*

Denying the Antecedent

As before, there is an argument that is superficially similar to *modus tollens,* but is actually a fallacy. It has this form:

1. If p, then q.
2. Not p.
3. Therefore, not q.

We can see that this is fallacious by substituting the phrases for the symbols:

1. If it is snowing, then it must be cold outside.
2. It is not snowing.
3. Therefore, it is not cold outside.

But clearly, it could be cold outside and still not snow. So the argument is invalid. Since the second premise denies that the antecedent (p) is true, this fallacy is called "denying the antecedent." Here are some examples:

1. If we found dinosaurs and humans next to each other in the same rock formation, then they must have lived at the same time.
2. We do not find them next to each other in the same rock formation.
3. Therefore, they did not live at the same time.

This denies the antecedent and is fallacious. There could be several reasons why dinosaur fossils are not normally found next to human fossils; perhaps dinosaurs and people typically did not live in the same area (as one hypothetical explanation).

1. If God were to perform a miracle in front of me right now, then that would prove He exists.
2. God is not performing a miracle in front of me right now.
3. Therefore, He doesn't exist.

Again, this denies the antecedent. God is under no obligation to perform a miracle at the whim of one of His creations. Nor is it likely that the atheist would accept a given miracle as legitimate anyway — preferring to trust that future studies will reveal that the event is explainable by natural law.

Summary Table

(1) If p, then q. (2) p. (3) Therefore, q.	valid: *modus ponens*
(1) If p, then q. (2) q. (3) Therefore, p.	fallacy of affirming the consequent
(1) If p, then q. (2) Not q. (3) Therefore, not p.	valid: *modus tollens*
(1) If p, then q. (2) Not p. (3) Therefore, not q.	fallacy of denying the antecedent

Addendum: "Probably . . ."

Some of the most-used arguments for evolution are nothing but the fallacy of affirming the consequent. It is very, very common. So it comes as no surprise that evolutionists are not happy with me for exposing the fallacious nature of such arguments. After an early version of this chapter was published on the Answers in Genesis website, some evolutionists tried to respond to it and defend their arguments in which they had affirmed the consequent. In several such responses, the evolutionists conceded that affirming the consequent is indeed a fallacy; but they claimed that since they were only arguing that evolution is highly likely to be true (not definitely true), they had not committed the fallacy. Essentially, they thought that they could extricate themselves by adding the word "probably" to their conclusion, transforming the argument to an inductive one. In other words, the argument becomes:

1. If evolution were true, we would expect to see similarities in DNA of all organisms on earth.
2. We do see similarities in DNA of all organisms on earth.
3. Therefore, evolution is **probably** true.

Does changing the argument to an inductive one really make it cogent? Let's try another example to see if "probably" will make the argument cogent:

1. If the moon is made of light bulbs, then it will be bright.
2. The moon is bright.
3. Therefore, the moon is **probably** made of light bulbs.

Clearly, adding "probably" to the conclusion of such a fallacy does not make the conclusion likely at all. So the evolutionists' arguments are *still* fallacious. Similarities in DNA and the existence of the cosmic microwave background do not provide cogent arguments for evolution or the big bang. Since the arguments become inductive, rather than deductive by adding "probably," they would most likely be classified as the fallacy of the hasty generalization (see chapter 11).

Yet scientists (doing real science in the present) do use something strikingly similar to affirming the consequent as part of their standard procedure. They form a hypothesis (p), which predicts a specific experimental result (q). They then perform an experiment or observation that affirms (or denies) q. If the prediction of the hypothesis is confirmed, doesn't this provide support for said hypothesis? Isn't that what the scientific method is all about? Yet this appears to be fallacious, leading us to ask: *Is the scientific method based on the fallacy of affirming the consequent?*

Secular philosophers have struggled over this very issue. Science does seem to be formally invalid, and yet, it is incredibly successful. How do we account for this? I submit that in the secular worldview, all science (be it operational science or "origins" science) is indeed fallacious; therefore, there is no rational explanation for the success of science, or justification for its continued use *within the secular worldview*. However, the Christian *can* answer this question.

In the Christian worldview, there is an underlying orderliness to the universe because God (who is beyond time, and not limited to space) upholds time and space in a consistent fashion for our benefit. Therefore, some things will be the same over time and space (the laws of physics, for example). Yet God allows for different conditions in different places and at different times. Therefore, some things will not be the same over time and space (such as *temperature*, for example). By performing a controlled experiment at many different times and places, we can learn to distinguish those things that are constant due to God's upholding power (laws of nature), from those things that change (local/temporal conditions). We can construct models that rely upon God's consistency, and then test those models under various conditions. Repeated success indicates that our model is more likely to be true than competitors with less success.

So in the Christian worldview, a scientific model that makes many specific, successful predictions under a variety of conditions, and that outperforms other competing models, is indeed likely to be a good approximation of the way the universe works. (Note that evolution does not really make any specific predictions, and the vague predictions it makes are also predicted by creation models — i.e., we'd expect to see similarities in DNA since God is the Designer of all life.) The scientific method makes sense in a biblical creation worldview, because we are relying on God's promise to uphold the universe in a consistent way in order to learn by experience. However, science cannot be justified on an evolutionary worldview because there is no basis for induction.[1]

Examples of Affirming the Consequent:

"If evolution were true, we would expect to find similarities in the DNA of all living organisms. And this is exactly what we find." [Unstated conclusion: "Therefore evolution is true, or very probably true." But of course, creationists would make the same prediction.]

"If fossils have been deposited over millions of years of evolution, then we would expect to find a progressive trend in the fossil record. And that is exactly what we find." [But worldwide flood models also predict a trend in the fossil record due to ecological zoning, mobility, etc. Organisms that lived lower (e.g., sea snails) are generally found lower than organisms that live high (e.g., birds.)]

"If the big bang were true, we'd expect to see a cosmic microwave background. Lo and behold, that's exactly what we find." ["Therefore, the big bang is (probably) true."]

"Evolution models predict X. X is true. Thus, evolution is (likely) true." [Such an argument is particularly fallacious when creation models also predict X.]

Examples of Denying the Antecedent

"If we found dinosaurs and humans in the same fossil layers, then that would prove they lived at the same time. But we don't find this." [Unstated conclusion: "They did not live at the same time."]

"If God were to perform a miracle right now in front of me, then I would believe that He exists. But I see no miracle in front of me. Thus, He does not exist."

"If we found a bunny in a Cambrian fossil bed, that would certainly prove that creation is true. But we find no such thing." [Conclusion: "Thus, creation isn't true." But creationists really wouldn't expect to find such a thing, since bunnies do not live on the ocean floor.]

"What would prove that creation is true? If we found the Bible written in English in the DNA of some organism then that would convince me. But of course we find no such thing." ["Thus, creation isn't true."]

Endnotes

1. For more information on this topic, see "Evolution: the Anti-Science" on the Answers in Genesis website, or the book *The Ultimate Proof of Creation* by Jason Lisle (Green Forest, AR: Master Books, 2009), chapter 3.

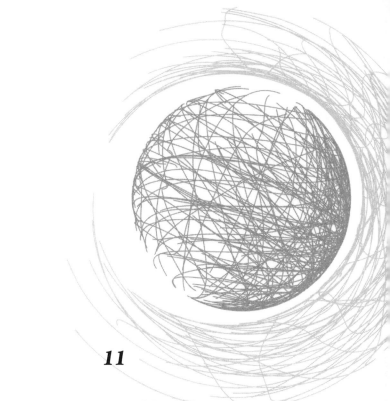

11

Other Fallacies

The previous chapters have covered what I believe to be the most common fallacies that occur in origins debates. And because they are so common, they deserved to be discussed in some detail. However, it is helpful to have some familiarity with less common fallacies as well. For that reason, I offer this additional chapter that briefly summarizes some of the less common fallacies that come up in debates. Though not as ubiquitous as the previous examples, these fallacies do occur often enough, so it is good to know how to spot and refute them.

> *Genetic fallacy*
> —
> *dismissing an argument because one objects to the source of the argument*

The Genetic Fallacy occurs when someone dismisses an argument because they object to the source of the argument. The most common examples of this in origins debates are when someone dismisses information contained in the Bible, or information that comes from another creation-based source.

If a creationist cites an article in the *Answers Research Journal* in support of a particular claim, it would be fallacious for the critic to respond, "Well, that's a *creationist* journal. Do you have any support from mainstream journals?" The response is truly absurd because, of course, secular (mainstream) journals would rarely publish an article that supports a conclusion contrary to the mainstream worldview. This doesn't mean that the creationist journal is in any way wrong, so the critic's response is utterly irrelevant. An argument should be evaluated on its merit, not its source. Now, if a source of information can be established as unreliable, then that certainly merits mentioning. However, this must be argued, and not simply taken for granted.

> **Fallacy of composition**
>
> —
>
> *arguing that what is true of the parts must also be true of the whole, or what is true of the members of a group is also true of the group*

The Fallacy of Composition occurs when a person fallaciously argues that what is true of the parts must also be true of the whole, or what is true of the members of a group is also true of the group. Sometimes this is indeed the case, but it is not always necessarily so; we must examine the argument on a case-by-case basis. For example: "A red brick is red, so a house made of red bricks will be red" is not fallacious. But to say, "A brick is not very heavy, therefore a house made of bricks is not very heavy," is the fallacy of composition. Creationists sometimes commit the fallacy when they argue, "Everything within the universe has a cause. Therefore, the universe must have a cause." This does not follow logically; it is the fallacy of composition.

The Fallacy of Division is arguing that what is true of the whole must also be true of the parts. It is essentially the opposite of the fallacy of composition. "A person is alive and is made of atoms, therefore atoms are alive" is an example of the fallacy of division.

> *Fallacy of division*
> —
> *arguing that what is true of the whole must also be true of the parts*

A Hasty Generalization is drawing a generalization from too few specific examples. Some friends of mine vacationed in Florida for a week, and it was unusually cold for the entire time of their visit. It would be a hasty generalization for them to conclude that Florida has a cold climate. Their experience was atypical. One week is simply not enough time to tell what the weather is generally like. Now, if I spent five years living in Florida, it would not be a hasty generalization for me to conclude that the weather is generally warm and humid.

> *Hasty generalization*
> —
> *drawing a generalization from too few specific examples*

Watch for the fallacy of the hasty generalization in origins debates. "Creationists are dishonest. I once knew this creationist who lied left and right" is a hasty generalization. Assuming that the critic's claim about this particular creationist is true, it does not follow that creationists are *generally* dishonest.

A Sweeping Generalization is applying a generalization to an exception. Generalizations are statements that generally — but not always — apply. They are meant to be true for most of their members, most of the time. But there are exceptions. "Jogging is good for the heart. Bill has a heart condition, so he should go jogging" is a sweeping generalization. Although jogging is generally good for the heart, there may be some cases where it could be dangerous.

> *Sweeping generalization*
> —
> *applying a generalization to an exception*

exception to the rule

Some examples of the sweeping generalization in origins debates are: "Nothing is true just because someone says it is. Therefore, you shouldn't just automatically trust what God has said in the Bible." Although it is generally true that nothing is true just because someone says it is, God is an exception because His Word defines truth. "Natural laws govern the operation of the universe. So you shouldn't invoke the supernatural to explain the origin of things in the universe" is another example of this fallacy. Although God normally accomplishes His will through natural laws, the creation of the universe is an exception to this generalization.

> The "No True Scotsman" fallacy
> —
> when an arguer defines a term in a biased way to protect his argument from rebuttals

The **"No True Scotsman Fallacy"** is when an arguer defines a term in a biased way (a definition that will not be found in a dictionary) to protect his argument from rebuttals. The example from which the name is taken is this: Person A asserts that no Scotsman puts sugar on his porridge. Person B refutes this claim by providing a counter-example: "Angus is a Scotsman — and he puts sugar on his porridge." But Person A responds by saying, "Ah, but no *true* Scotsman puts sugar on his porridge." He has essentially redefined the term "Scotsman" in such a way that his original claim cannot be wrong. But since this definition is fallacious, so is his argument.

This comes up in origins debates quite frequently:

Evolutionist: "No scientist believes that God created everything in six days."

Creationist: "The scientists at Answers in Genesis believe that God created in six days."

Evolutionist: "Well, no *real* scientist believes that God created in six days."

Special Pleading is the fallacy of applying a double standard. This occurs when a person expects his opponent to abide by a particular

petitio examptra

> **Special pleading**
> —
> *fallacy of applying a double standard*

standard when he himself does not. Almost all evolutionists insist that creationists should have a good reason for their position. Yet, evolutionists themselves do not have a good reason to believe in evolution — or induction, objective morality, or laws of logic.

A False Analogy occurs when the arguer makes a comparison between two things that are alike in only trivial ways, irrelevant to the argument. One of the most common examples (which I hear all the time) is, "Believing in creation is like believing in a flat earth." The arguer is trying to link creation with a belief that can be demonstrated to be false by observation. However, biblical creation has not been falsified by observation. For that matter, the Bible teaches that the earth is round (Job 26:10; Isa. 40:22). So the analogy fails.

> **False analogy**
> —
> *making a comparison between two things that are alike in only trivial ways, irrelevant to the argument*

The Fallacy of False Cause is when a person attributes a false cause-and-effect relationship between two events. Just because two things happen at about the same time does not mean that one has caused the other. It could simply be a coincidence, or there could be a third factor that has caused both events. You may sometimes hear a critic claim that Christianity caused the Dark Ages, or that the discovery of evolution is responsible for modern medical science and technology. Both of these are examples of the fallacy of false cause. A particular type of this fallacy is called the *post hoc ergo propter hoc*, which means "after this, therefore because of this." An example would be: "We started allowing creation to be taught in our science classes, and the test scores dropped. So do you see

> **Fallacy of false cause**
> —
> *attributing a false cause-and-effect relationship between two events*

Correlation

(Guilt by association)

what teaching creation does?" The argument is fallacious because there could be a number of reasons why test scores dropped. Just because event B happens after event A does not mean that A *caused* B.

Slippery slope fallacy

—

arguing that a particular action will set off an undesirable chain of events, when in reality other factors would tend to prevent such a result

The Slippery Slope Fallacy occurs when a person argues that a particular action will set off an undesirable chain of events, when in reality other factors would tend to prevent such a result. For example, "If we allow for the possibility of miracles, then science will come to a halt! We'd never know if we are studying a law of nature or an act of God." However, miracles are rare (by definition).[1] So science will not come to a halt by allowing for the possibility that God may occasionally (and temporarily) suspend a law of nature. Another example, "If students are taught creation in schools, they won't be able to do science when they are older." Presumably, this kind of thinking stems from the first example: that science cannot allow for the supernatural. But since this isn't the case, the arguer's conclusion does not follow.

Fallacy of irrelevant thesis

—

proving a point, but not the point at issue

The Fallacy of Irrelevant Thesis occurs when an arguer does prove a point, but it is not the point at issue. His assertion (though possibly true) is utterly irrelevant to the claim he is attempting to prove. Evolutionists often commit this fallacy when attempting to counter the evidence of design in the universe. For example, "Why is the universe so ideally suitable for life? It's not God. It's because if it were not suitable for life, we wouldn't be here to observe it." It is quite true that if the universe were not ideally suitable for life we wouldn't be here to observe it. But that is utterly irrelevant to the question at issue: namely, *why* is the universe so well-suited for life? To see why this fails, consider the following analogy.

lets unpack that
lets disentangle that

Suppose I was the sole survivor of an airplane crash. When a reporter asks me how it was that I was able to survive, it would be fallacious for me to reply, "Because if I hadn't survived, I would not be here to answer your question." Although it is true that I would not be around to answer the question had I died, this really doesn't answer the question itself — *why* I was able to survive. All fallacies of irrelevant thesis can be rebutted with this simple phrase: "True perhaps, but irrelevant."

When evolutionists argue, "Life only *appears* to be designed by intelligence because if it weren't so well-organized it wouldn't have survived until now," this is the fallacy of irrelevant thesis. "The reason that organisms are well-suited to their environment has nothing to do with design. It is explained by natural selection." This is the fallacy of irrelevant thesis because natural selection only explains why we do *not* find organisms that are *not* suited for their environment (i.e., because they die). Natural selection does *not* actually explain why we *do* find organisms that are well-suited to their environment. The answer for this is that God created the initial organisms with sufficient information in their DNA to produce traits that would allow them to survive in a particular environment. This particular example occurs quite frequently; so study the above example carefully and be ready to discuss it when it comes up.

Faulty Appeals are a class of informal logical fallacies where the arguer tries to support his or her conclusion by appealing to something that is irrelevant to the claim at issue. We have already covered one of the fallacies in this category: the faulty appeal to authority was dealt with in an earlier chapter. But there are several other faulty appeals in this category. While not nearly as common as the faulty appeal to authority, these other fallacies do sometimes come up in origins debates.

The Appeal to Force/Fear is the fallacy of arguing for a position on the basis that negative consequences will follow if a person does not accept the position. Basically, this fallacy is like saying, "You better accept my claim, or else there will be consequences!" But of course, whether or not such consequences would follow is utterly irrelevant to the claim at issue. It is surprising that anyone would fall for such an obvious fallacy. Yet the appeal to force is becoming increasingly

legitimate use

warn a child or toll of consequ of sin! And so to ignore would place self in enormous danger

> ⬦⬦⬦⬦⬦⬦⬦⬦⬦⬦⬦⬦⬦⬦⬦⬦⬦⬦⬦⬦
>
> ### *The appeal to force/fear*
>
> —
>
> *arguing for a position on the basis that negative consequences will follow if a person does not accept the position*
>
> ⬦⬦⬦⬦⬦⬦⬦⬦⬦⬦⬦⬦⬦⬦⬦⬦⬦⬦⬦⬦

common among evolution activists. For example, a creationist professor may be denied tenure simply for believing in creation. Another example, "If you teach creation in this school, we'll sue you." Any time legal action is threatened for believing/teaching creation it is the fallacy of the appeal to force. It is an utterly irrational approach to persuasion. As Copi and Cohen state, "The appeal to force is the abandonment of reason."[2]

> ⬦⬦⬦⬦⬦⬦⬦⬦⬦⬦⬦⬦⬦⬦⬦⬦⬦⬦⬦⬦
>
> ### *Appeal to emotion*
>
> —
>
> *fallacy of attempting to persuade people by stirring powerful emotions rather than making a logical case.*
>
> ⬦⬦⬦⬦⬦⬦⬦⬦⬦⬦⬦⬦⬦⬦⬦⬦⬦⬦⬦⬦

The Appeal to Emotion is the fallacy of attempting to persuade people by stirring powerful emotions rather than making a logical case. A stirring speech may bring about thunderous applause from the audience, even though no logical case has been made. As another example, an evolutionist may chide a creationist by saying, "If you really believe the Bible then I suppose you believe in slavery and stoning rebellious children as the Bible teaches." This is fallacious because the critic is attempting to stir an emotional reaction (rather than making an argument) by tapping into our cultural aversion to brutal slavery and our opinions of harsh penalties.

In fact, the biblical slavery system is nothing like the brutal images that are conjured in the modern American's mind due to our nation's history. Rather, biblical "slavery" was a very generous system that was designed to help irresponsible people get out of debt and become financially responsible. Moreover, the stoning of rebellious sons only applied to incorrigibles who (despite repeated discipline) continued to act brutally and bring harm to their parents and others. By falsely associating modern conceptions of these things with the Bible, the evolutionist is attempting to persuade people by stirring emotions, not by making a logical argument.

The Appeal to Pity is a particular type of the appeal to emotion and occurs when an arguer tries to persuade people to accept a position by generating sympathy for those who hold the position. An atheistic evolutionist might talk about how he was mistreated by creationists, or how difficult it was for him to grow up in an area with many Christians. Even if these things are true, it is utterly irrelevant to the truth of his position. The absurdity of the appeal to pity is perhaps best illustrated in the old tale of the boy who killed both of his parents with an ax. When it was clear that he was going to be found guilty of the crime, he pleaded for leniency on the grounds that he was an orphan!

> *Appeal to pity*
> —
> *persuading people to accept a position by generating sympathy for those who hold the position*

The Appeal to Ignorance is the fallacy of appealing to the unknown; specifically, it is when a person argues that a claim is probably true simply because it has never been proven false. For example, "There must be life in outer space. After all, no one has proven that there isn't." Of course, just because something cannot be proved false does not mean that it is true. An appeal to ignorance is always arbitrary. As such, it is always reversible. I could respond to the above example by saying, "Well, there must *not* be life in outer space. After all, no one has proven that there is."

> *Appeal to ignorance*
> —
> *fallacy of appealing to the unknown; specifically when a person argues that a claim is probably true simply because it has never been proven false*

The Naturalistic Fallacy confuses what *is* with what *should be*. Specifically, the person committing this fallacy argues that since something is a particular way, it is morally acceptable for it to be that way. As an example, "Lots of people smoke, so it can't be wrong." The argument

83

> *Naturalistic fallacy*
>
> —
>
> *arguing that since something is a particular way, it is morally acceptable for it to be that way*

is fallacious because the way things are is not always the way things should be. This fallacy often comes up in origins debates when dealing with matters of morality. I have often pointed out that an absolute objective moral code is without foundation in an evolutionary worldview. But some evolutionists have responded by saying, "A moral code has survival value for the species. So that explains why we have morality." Although (for argument's sake) this might account for why people *do* behave in a particular way, it does not explain why people *should* behave in a particular way.

The **Moralistic Fallacy** also confuses what *is* with what *should be*, but in the opposite direction. The arguer asserts that because something should be a particular way, it is that particular way. If you have ever crossed an intersection when the light says "walk" without looking both ways, you have implicitly committed this fallacy; you have reasoned that since it is *wrong* for a driver

> *Moralistic fallacy*
>
> —
>
> *asserting that because something should be a particular way, it is a particular way*

to run a red light, the drivers *will* not run the red light. But that isn't necessarily so. For example, "No creationist has ever been fired just for believing in creation. That would be wrong."

> *"Fallacy" fallacy*
>
> —
>
> *assuming that a claim is false simply because an argument for that position is fallacious*

The **"Fallacy Fallacy"** is the error of assuming that a claim is false simply because an argument for that position is fallacious. A bad argument can still have a true conclusion "by accident." For example, "I was sick and I prayed to God. I got better. Therefore, God does exist." This is a fallacious argument (it is a form of affirming the consequent). However, if another person responded, "That's a bad argument for God. So God does not exist," then he would be committing the fallacy fallacy. Usually the conclusion is only implied; if it were directly stated, the fallacy would be obvious. I've seen this fallacy occur in origins debates when an evolutionist chides a creationist for using a bad argument, and then uses this as evidence for evolution. It's unfortunate that an evolutionist would argue this way, but it is even more disappointing that a creationist would use a fallacious argument in the first place.

Concluding Remarks

It is the obligation of the Christian to be rational — to pattern our thinking after God's (Isa. 55:7–8). We are to be imitators of Him (Eph. 5:1) and to think in a way that is consistent with God's logical nature (Rom. 12:2). Not only do we belong to God as His creations, but He has redeemed us by His Son. Our commitment to Christ, therefore, must extend to all aspects of our life. We are to love the Lord with all our heart, soul, strength, and mind (Luke 10:27).

I hope that you have enjoyed this book on evolution and logical fallacies and that the information presented here will help in your defense of the faith. For more information on defending the Christian faith, consider reading *The Ultimate Proof of Creation*, which will give you an absolutely irrefutable argument for the Christian worldview. A good textbook on logic or logical fallacies may also be helpful, even if it is not written from a Christian perspective.[3] Christian apologist Dr. Greg Bahnsen also has a lecture series on logic and critical thinking that may be very helpful and is available from the Covenant Media Foundation, www.cmfnow.com.

I would also suggest going through one or more of the "tests" provided in chapters 12 and 14 (with answer keys in chapters 13 and 15 respectively). Like most other things in life, the most effective way to learn to spot fallacies is practice, practice, practice.

Endnotes

1. Moreover, a miracle is not *necessarily* outside of natural law. God can do extraordinary things by natural laws if He so chooses. The point is this: if God does occasionally work outside of natural law, it will certainly not bring science to a halt.

2. I.M. Copi and C. Cohen, *Introduction to Logic*, 10th edition (Upper Saddle River, NJ: Prentice Hall, 1994), p.172.

3. Ibid. This is an excellent textbook on logic. I also recommend *With Good Reason* by S. Morris Engel (Boston, MA: Bedford/St. Martin's, 2000), which is a book on informal fallacies.

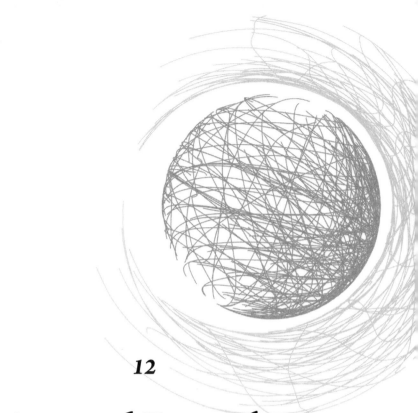

12

Assorted Examples

T hese hypothetical examples are based primarily on the types of
common errors in reasoning committed in arguments for evolution or in other religious conversations. The goal is to identify
the main fallacy in each. An answer key is provided in chapter 13.

1. "Evolution has designed some amazing creatures."

2. "It's a scientific fact that bacteria have evolved resistance to various antibiotics, so creationists are wrong to say that evolution has
   not been observed."

3. "Why are you creationists against scientific progress?"

4. "Evolution is a scientific fact; virtually all the top scientists believe
   in it."

5. "If evolution is true, then we'd expect that organisms that look similar would have similar DNA. And this is exactly what we find, so evolution must be true."

6. "Either you live by faith, or you have rational reasons for what you believe."

7. "God does not exist. After all, He kills innocent children; clearly that's not right."

8. "If fossils of humans and dinosaurs were found together, then we'd know they coexisted. But no such fossils have been found. So clearly they didn't live at the same time."

9. "Creation is so stupid it's not even worth debating it."

10. "Creationists are dishonest, so I wouldn't rely on any of their arguments."

11. "Today, we will be debating science vs. creationism."

12. "99.99% of scientists in relevant fields believe in evolution."

13. "You want an example of evolution? You're speaking with one."

14. "Science tells us that the universe is billions of years old."

15. "If Genesis is true, then why is there so much evidence for an old earth?"

16. "Creationists try to find answers in the Bible, but real scientists do research to find out what happened in the past."

17. "My latest book is about the evolution vs. creationism controversy."

18. "Creationists take the Bible literally. They must believe the earth has corners and pillars. How absurd!"

19. "The fossil record shows that some organisms are systematically found higher in the strata than others. This is clear evidence for evolution."

20. "Of course Dr. Lisle believes in creation. He works at Answers in Genesis!"

21. "If students are not taught evolution, they will not understand how science really works, and will be deprived of a proper understanding of nature."

22. "Evolution is an inescapable fact. Everything in the universe, from stars and galaxies to finch beaks and bacteria, is in a constant state of evolution."

23. "In the future, we expect that nature will be uniform because it has been that way in the past."

24. "To deny that evolution takes place would be like denying the existence of gravity."

25. "Either you use your brain to determine what's true, or you simply accept whatever the Bible says."

26. "Evolution is science. And science is why we have such incredible technology today, and can put men on the moon."

27. "Evolution is *not* an unguided process. Rather, evolution is guided by natural selection. Nature selects individuals that are most fit, thus driving the process forward."

28. "You are really stupid if you believe in creation."

29. "You shouldn't believe in or teach creation here; you might get sued."

30. "Why do you deny science?"

31. "If we found fossil rabbits in the Precambrian, that would certainly disprove evolution. But such a thing has never been found. So we can have confidence that evolution is true."

32. "You should not trust anything that is posted on the Answers in Genesis website."

33. "Well, of course Dr. Dave is going to argue for a young earth. He believes in creation. So you shouldn't accept his argument."

34. "The synapses of the brain must have at least some degree of consciousness, since the brain is made up of these synapses and is conscious."

35. "People just don't come back to life. Go check out a cemetery. So it just isn't possible for Jesus to have been raised from the dead."

36. "You don't need God to account for laws of logic. I don't even believe in God, and I use logic all the time."

37. "Clearly, it is not wrong to abort babies. People have been doing it for thousands of years."

38. "Interracial marriage is wrong. You don't see sparrows mating with cardinals."

39. "If students are taught to simply 'trust in the Bible,' they won't be able to think for themselves, and will not be able to function in society when they grow up."

40. "What is the probability that life could arise by chance? It must be 100 percent because we are here, after all."

41. "No, evolutionists are not lying about all the evidence for evolution. After all, that would be wrong."

42. "If evolution is not true, then why do so many scientists accept it?"

43. "Darwin documented evolution in action by noting how the beaks of finches responded to changes in the environment."

44. "Essentially, all mammals have seven vertebrae in their neck. This is just one of many evidences of the fact that they share a common ancestor."

45. "If you are going to make an argument for creation, you have to use real, mainstream journals, not creationist ones."

46. "The only reason you believe in creation is because you are a Christian."

47. "The Oort cloud clearly must exist. No one has any proof that it doesn't."

48. "All the classic arguments for God have been refuted. This certainly suggests that God does not exist."

49. "Science is all about what is observable and testable. That's why creation cannot be taken seriously. There is simply no way to observe it or test it."

50. "You can't use circular reasoning in your arguments — that's fallacious. So you cannot assume the Bible is true while you are attempting to prove it."

51. "Do you believe in creation, or do you believe in science?"

52. "Of course creation cannot be true. Science is limited to the study of the natural world. But creation involves the supernatural."

53. "God may exist. But we must do science as if He does not. Otherwise, we would never know if we are studying the natural world, or a miracle. Science would come to a standstill."

54. "We allowed the students to discuss alternatives to evolution this year and the science test scores were below normal. Do you see what allowing creationist ideas into the classroom does?"

55. "Human beings cannot have any genuine free will. After all, we are made up entirely of atoms, which have no free will."

56. "Throughout history, we have consistently found natural explanations for various cosmic and terrestrial phenomena. So, it is reasonable to conclude that the origin of the universe and earth also has a natural cause."

57. "Life is abundant on earth; almost every possible environment is filled with living organisms. So it is reasonable to conclude that life in space is also quite common."

58. "Creationists do not believe in the scientific method. They simply look to the Bible for all the answers."

59. "The evidence for evolution is simply overwhelming. Evidence from genetics, from paleontology, from anatomy, all support the fact that all organisms share a common ancestor."

60. "Isn't evolution wonderful? The majesty of the eagle, the incredible speed of the cheetah, the ingenious color-changing ability

of the chameleon, and the splendor of a peacock feather are all glorious outcomes of one of nature's most amazing and intricate processes."

61. "We don't know if birds evolved from the ground up or from the trees down."

62. "I think, therefore I am."

Common Creationist Fallacies

63. "God changed my life. So of course He exists."

64. "I know God still heals people today because I prayed to God when I was sick, and I got better."

65. "You want proof that the Bible is true and inspired by God? Okay, 2 Timothy 3:16."

66. "Everything within the universe has a cause. So clearly the universe must be caused."

67. "I have a very good argument for creation; I know it is sound because every evolutionist I've used the argument on has converted to believing in creation."

68. "You ask me how I know He lives. He lives within my heart."

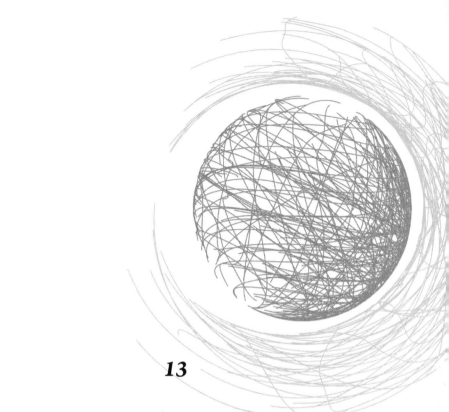

13

Assorted Examples — Answers

1. **Reification:** Evolution is a concept and as such it cannot design anything.

2. **Equivocation:** The arguer has shifted the meaning of the word "evolution."

3. **Complex Question:** The question assumes something untrue. It should be divided: "Are you against scientific progress? And if so, why?"

4. **Appeal to Authority:** The fact that some scientists believe something doesn't necessarily make it so.

5. **Affirming the Consequent:** There are other reasons to expect that organisms would have similar DNA. They have a common Creator, and their DNA has instructions for traits.

6. **Bifurcations:** We can have faith *and* have rational reasons for what we believe.

7. **Irrelevant Thesis:** The fact that God does things that some people do not understand or find displeasing does not disprove God's existence.

8. **Denying the Antecedent:** There could be a number of reasons why dinosaur fossils are not typically found with humans; the answer need not be a separation in time.

9. **Question-begging Epithet:** Emotional/biased language is used in place of an argument.

10. **Abusive *Ad Hominem*:** The attack is directed against the person's character, not his argument.

11. **Question-begging Epithet:** By contrasting creation with science, the person is implying that creation is somehow contrary to science, or that evolution is the scientific view, without making a logical argument for this. The "-ism" attached to "creation" further reinforces the claim that creation is merely a "belief."

12. **Faulty Appeal to Authority/Majority:** Even if the number were correct (which it is not), it would be irrelevant to the correctness of the claim.

13. **Begging the Question:** That people are an example of evolution is the very claim at issue. This person merely asserts evolution as his defense of evolution.

14. **Reification:** Science is personified, which conceals the biases of the scientists who are actually making such a claim.

15. **Complex Question:** This should be divided: "Is there much evidence for an old earth? If so, how can Genesis be true?" But the

biblical creationist would answer no to the first question, so the second question is not meaningful.

16. **"No True Scotsman" Fallacy:** The arguer is trying to protect his claim from counterargument by defining a "*real* scientist" as one who does not look to the Bible.

17. **Question-begging Epithet:** The "-ism" on "creation" is the give-away. This person is suggesting that creation is merely a belief, whereas evolution is factual, without making an argument for this.

18. **Strawman Argument** or **Equivocation:** Creationists do not take the Bible in a wooden-literal sense. We do allow for figures of speech and poetic language in those parts of the Bible that are written that way. This could also be considered equivocation on the word *literally*, which can simply mean "naturally" (in the sense the author intended), but is shifted to mean strictly concretely.

19. **Affirming the Consequent:** (Other answers are possible too.) When put in standard form, the arguer is implying: Evolution predicts X. We observe X, therefore, evolution is true.

20. **Circumstantial *Ad Hominem*:** The fact that a person is motivated to make an argument has no bearing on the soundness of that argument.

21. **Appeal to Pity:** The word *deprived* may give away the emotional appeal implied in this argument. But the idea "teach evolution or the children will suffer" has no bearing on whether evolution is true.

22. **Equivocation:** (On the word *evolution*)

23. **Begging the Question:** The arguer is assuming induction to prove induction. (See chapter 3.)

24. **Fallacy of False Analogy:** Gravity is observable, testable, and repeatable in the present, unlike particles-to-people evolution.

25. **Bifurcation:** Why not use our brain to reason from the Bible as our starting point?

26. **Equivocation:** The arguer conflates a particular model of origins science with operational science.

27. **Fallacy of Reification:** Natural selection/Nature is conceptual and does not actually guide anything.

28. **Abusive *Ad Hominem*:** The argument is directed at the person, not the claim.

29. **Appeal to Force/Fear:** That legal action might result is irrelevant to the truth of creation.

30. **Complex Question:** It should be divided: "Do you deny science? If so, why?" Since the first answer is no, the second question isn't needed.

31. **Denying the Antecedent:** (If p then q, not p therefore not q.) Creationists would not expect to find rabbits in the Precambrian either, since it is thought to be essentially the pre-Flood ocean floor.

32. **Genetic Fallacy:** An argument should be evaluated on its merit, not its source. Furthermore, a source must be established as faulty by good reasons if we are to argue that its claims should not be trusted.

33. **Circumstantial *Ad Hominem*:** The fact that Dr. Dave is motivated to make an argument does not mean that his argument is unsound.

34. **Fallacy of Division:** What is true of the whole is not necessarily true of the parts.

35. **Sweeping Generalization:** Most people don't come back to life (not yet anyway). So the generalization is true. But that doesn't mean that there are no exceptions. God can indeed raise the dead, and has done so.

36. **Fallacy of Irrelevant Thesis:** The creationist claim is that laws of logic require the existence of the biblical God (*not* a profession of belief in God). So the atheist's point may be true, but is totally irrelevant. It does not refute the creationist claim.

37. **Naturalistic Fallacy:** Just because something *is* a particular way does not mean that it *should be* that way. The fact that many people abort babies does not make it right.

38. **Fallacy of False Analogy:** People are not (biblically) in the same category as animals. How animals behave is not necessarily how people are supposed to behave. Some animals kill and eat their own kind.

39. **Slippery Slope Fallacy:** Since trusting in the Bible does involve proper reasoning skills (e.g., Isa. 1:18), it will not lead to the undesirable chain of events suggested by the critic.

40. **Begging the Question:** Since the way we got here is the very claim at issue, the arguer has merely assumed what he is attempting to prove.

41. **Moralistic Fallacy:** Just because something would be wrong does not mean that it will not happen.

42. **Faulty Appeal to Authority/Majority:** People have a sin nature and, as such, do not always draw the most reasonable conclusion given the data.

43. **Equivocation:** The "evolution in action" noted by the arguer is simply change within a kind. It is not "evolution" in the particles-to-people sense, which is what he is presumably trying to assert.

44. **Affirming the Consequent** or **False Cause:** The form of the argument is "If evolution is true, then X. X is true, therefore evolution is true." This affirms the consequent. Though evolutionists do expect similarities in major groups of organisms, so do creationists. It is the cause of that similarity that is the point at issue.

45. **No True Scotsman Fallacy** or **Special Pleading:** The term "real" implies that creationist journals do not count, thereby defining "journal" in a biased way — the no true Scotsman fallacy. Moreover, if he is going to insist that the creationist use only journals opposite to the creationist's position, then why will he not abide by that standard, too? To be fair, we could ask the evolutionist to use only creationist journals to make his argument, not evolutionist ones.

46. **Circumstantial *Ad Hominem*:** Being a Christian does motivate (and cause) the person to believe in creation. However, this is irrelevant to whether the Christian has a good argument for creation.

47. **The Appeal to Ignorance:** Such a fallacy is always reversible. We could respond, "Well, then there must *not* be an Oort cloud; no one has any proof that it does exist."

48. **The "Fallacy Fallacy":** The fact that an argument for a claim is faulty does not mean that the claim is necessarily false.

49. **Special Pleading:** Evolution is also not observable or testable in the present. Yet, the arguer considers it to be scientific. He is exempting his own position from the criteria used to dismiss the creation position. He is using a double standard.

50. **Special Pleading** and **Begging the Question:** The Bible teaches that all knowledge is in Christ (Col. 2:3), thus we must stand on the Bible even when defending it. The arguer is saying that this is wrong. He is therefore assuming that the Bible is wrong in his argument that the Bible is wrong. He is reasoning in a circle (begging the question), and then telling the creationist not to reason in a circle. This is special pleading.

51. **Bifurcation:** Why not both?

52. **Fallacy of Irrelevant Thesis:** Whether or not creation is classified as "science" is totally irrelevant to whether or not it is true.

53. **Slippery Slope Fallacy:** Since miracles (whether they involve a temporary suspension of the laws of nature or not) are rare by definition, we could easily distinguish a miracle from the normal flow of nature. Thus, science would not come to a halt.

54. **Fallacy of False Cause —** *post hoc ergo propter hoc*: That the lower test scores happened after the event does not mean that they were *caused* by the event.

55. **Fallacy of Composition:** The properties of the parts are not necessarily the same as the properties of the whole. (An airplane is composed of non-flying parts.)

56. **Sweeping Generalization** and **Fallacy of Composition:** Most but not all events in the universe do have a natural cause. But the creation of the universe is an exception (sweeping generalization). Moreover, just because (most of) the objects within the universe have a natural cause does not mean the universe as a whole has a natural cause (fallacy of composition).

57. **Hasty Generalization:** The earth is the exceptional case. So extrapolating the exception to form a rule is a hasty generalization.

58. **Strawman Fallacy:** Creationists do believe in the scientific method. In fact, only the Bible can account for science since science is based on induction. (See chapter 3.)

59. **Question-begging Epithet:** No argument is presented. The person simply uses biased language to assert his case.

60. **Appeal to Emotion** and **Question-begging Epithet:** The arguer uses emotive language to persuade the reader, not logic.

61. **Bifurcation:** The third unstated option is that birds were created.

62. **Begging the Question:** When Descartes said, "I think," he had already presupposed his own existence, which he then used to conclude his existence: "therefore I am."

63. **Begging the Question:** The statement "God changed my life" presupposes that God exists, which is the conclusion of the argument.

64. **False Cause –** *post hoc ergo propter hoc* **and Affirming the Consequent:** That God was the cause of the improvement has not been argued, just assumed since one came after the other. So this is a *post hoc ergo proper hoc* fallacy. When put into formal structure, the argument affirms the consequent: "If God still heals people then I will get better. I did get better, therefore God still heals people."

65. **Begging the Question:** This argument merely assumes the truth of the Bible in order to argue for it. It is an *arbitrary* form of circular reasoning, and is thus fallacious.

66. **Fallacy of Composition:** The properties of the parts are not necessarily the properties of the whole. (A house made of tiny atoms is not tiny.)

67. **Fallacy of Irrelevant Thesis:** The fact that an argument may persuade people does not in any way prove that the argument is sound.

68. **Begging the Question:** The premise presupposes the conclusion.

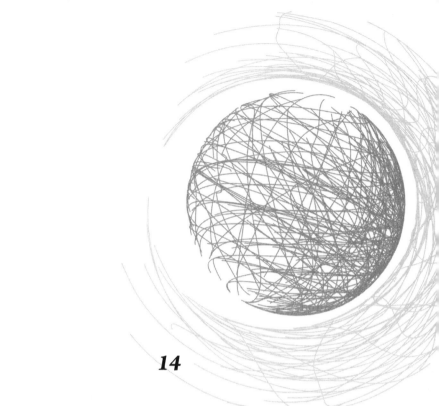

14

Real-world Examples

The examples used previously are hypothetical, though they are based on actual fallacies that I have encountered in evolutionary literature and conversations with evolutionists. Sometimes in real-world conversations, the fallacy is not quite so obvious. Most everyday arguments consist of "enthymemes." An enthymeme is an argument where a premise or the conclusion is left unstated because it is obvious. For example: "Scientists are supposed to be objective. And you are a scientist, aren't you?" The unstated conclusion is clear: "Therefore, you are supposed to be objective." In ordinary real-world conversations, we must think through what the critic is saying, *and* what he or she is *implying*.

Additionally, everyday arguments can contain more than one fallacy. Depending on what you take to be the main point of the argument, you might spot a different fallacy than someone else. Or, you may not see the argument as fallacious at all. There is a degree of subjectivity when we deal with real-world examples. All of the following examples are from evolutionary publications. In these publications, the authors are attempting to persuade the reader that evolution is true, that it is an important concept in science, and that there are no reasonable alternatives (particularly creation). So, you should evaluate the statements in light of that context. I suggest that you use these examples to test yourself. I have provided an "answer key" in chapter 15, but keep in mind that there is a degree of subjectivity in terms of which fallacy is most obvious.

1. "In public discussions of evolution and creationism, we are sometimes told by creationists and opponents of religion alike that we must choose between belief in creation and acceptance of the theory of evolution, between religion and science."[1]

2. "Science has boosted living standards, has enabled humans to travel into earth's orbit and to the moon, and has given us new ways of thinking about ourselves and the universe. Evolutionary biology has been and continues to be a cornerstone of modern science."[2]

3. "The rapid advances now being made in the life sciences and in medicine rest on principles derived from an understanding of evolution."[3]

4. "And it explains why nonscientific alternatives to evolution such as creationism (including intelligent design creationism) should not be part of the science curriculum in the nation's public schools."[4]

5. "But there is no controversy in the scientific community about whether evolution has occurred."[5]

6. "On the contrary, the evidence supporting descent with modification, as Charles Darwin termed it, is both overwhelming and compelling."[6]

7. "Biological evolution refers to changes in the traits of organisms over multiple generations."[7]

8. "An understanding of evolution was essential in the identification of the SARS virus. The genetic material in the virus was similar to that of other viruses because it had evolved from the same ancestor virus."[8]

9. "Many scientific theories are so well established that no new evidence is likely to alter them substantially. For example, no new evidence will demonstrate that the earth does not orbit around the sun (heliocentric theory). . . . Like these other foundational scientific theories, the theory of evolution is supported by so many observations and confirming experiments. . . ."[9]

10. "The evolutionary biologists who discovered *Tiktaalik* [see page 2] predicted that they would find fossils intermediate between fish and limbed terrestrial animals in sediments that were about 375 million years old. Their discovery confirmed the prediction made on the basis of evolutionary theory."[10]

11. "Because the evidence supporting it is so strong, scientists no longer question whether biological evolution has occurred and is continuing to occur."[11]

12. "The atomic structure of matter, the genetic basis of heredity, the circulation of blood, gravitation and planetary motion, and the process of biological evolution by natural selection are just a few examples of a very large number of scientific explanations that have been overwhelmingly substantiated."[12]

13. "Scientists and theologians have written eloquently about their awe and wonder at the history of the universe and of life on this planet, explaining that they see no conflict between their faith in God and the evidence for evolution." [In a section explaining why evolution can be compatible with religious faith.][13]

14. [In support of the big bang]:"Later observations with satellites showed that the background radiation in the universe has exactly the properties that would be predicted from the Big Bang."[14]

15. "According to modern cosmology, the particles that constitute ordinary matter (protons, neutrons, and electrons) formed when the universe cooled after the Big Bang."[15]

16. "Evidence from the most ancient fossils reveals that life has existed on earth for most of our planet's history"[16]

17. "Nevertheless, all organisms share some common traits because they all share common ancestors at some point in the past."[17]

18. "The bones in the forelimbs of terrestrial and some aquatic vertebrates are remarkably similar because they have all evolved from the forelimbs of a common ancestor."[18]

19. "Another compelling feature of the fossil record is its consistency. Nowhere on earth are fossils from dinosaurs, which went extinct 65 million years ago, found together with fossils from humans, who evolved in just the last few million years."[19]

20. "Nowhere are the fossils of mammals found in sediments that are more than about 220 million years old."[20]

21. "We are about to enter a century in which the United States will be even more dependent on science and technology than it has been in the past. . . . Yet the teaching of science in the nation's public schools often is marred by a serious omission. Many students receive little or no exposure to the most important concept in modern biology, a concept essential to understanding key aspects of living things — biological evolution."[21]

22. "More than one-half of Americans say that they would like to have creationism taught in public school classrooms — even though the Supreme Court has ruled that 'creation science' is a religious idea and that its teaching cannot be mandated in the public schools."[22]

23. "All living things use the same biochemical system to pass genetic information from one generation to another. From a scientific standpoint, there is one compelling answer to questions about life's commonalities. Different kinds of organisms share so many characteristics of structure and function because they are related to one another."[23]

24. "Though humans, fish, and bacteria would seem to be so different as to defy comparison, they all share some of the characteristics of their common ancestors."[24]

25. "In short, biological evolution accounts for three of the most fundamental features of the world around us: the similarities among living things, the diversity of life, and many features of the physical world we inhabit."[25]

26. "To teach biology without explaining evolution deprives students of a powerful concept that brings great order and coherence to our understanding of life."[26]

27. "Evolution explains why many human pathogens have been developing resistance to formerly effective drugs and suggests ways of confronting this increasingly serious problem"[27]

28. "However, there is no debate within the scientific community over whether evolution occurred, and there is no evidence that evolution has not occurred."[28]

29. "The central feature of this revolution has been the abandonment of one notion about stability after another: . . . that the world's living things are unchangeable, that the continents of the earth are held rigidly in place, and so on. . . . To accept the probability of change — and to see change as an agent of opportunity rather than as a threat — is a silent message and challenge in the lesson of evolution."[29]

30. "Teaching biology without evolution would be like teaching civics and never mentioning the United States Constitution."[30]

31. "The debate in science is over some of the details of how evolution occurred, not whether evolution happened or not."[31]

32. "A lot of science and science education organizations have made statements about why it is important to teach evolution."[32]

33. "We accept evolution as the best scientific explanation for a lot of observations — about fossils and biochemistry and evolutionary changes we can actually see, like how bacteria become resistant to certain medicines."[33]

34. "Scientists have looked at the arguments [for creation] and have found they are not supported by verifiable data."[34]

35. "Fossils of primitive microorganisms show that life had emerged on earth by about 3.8 billion years ago."[35]

36. "Similarly, the fossil record reveals profound changes in the kinds of living things that have inhabited our planet over its long history."[36]

37. [In dealing with the fact that scientists have discovered that mutations can cause variations in expressed traits]: "They showed that all variations, both slight and dramatic, arose through changes, or mutations, in genes."[37]

38. "Almost immediately, it became clear that certain proteins that serve the same function in different species have very similar amino acid sequences. The protein evidence was completely consistent with the idea of a common evolutionary history for the planet's living things."[38]

39. "This uniformity in the genetic code is powerful evidence for the interrelatedness of living things, suggesting that all organisms presently alive share a common ancestor that can be traced back to the origins of life on earth."[39]

40. "Natural selection tests the combinations of genes represented in the members of a species and allows to proliferate those that confer the greatest ability to survive and reproduce."[40]

41. [In response to "no one has ever seen evolution occur"]: "Scientific conclusions are not limited to direct observation but often depend on inferences that are made by applying reason to observations." [On the same page, in explaining why creation is not science]: "But science cannot test supernatural possibilities. . . . Because such appeals to the supernatural are not testable using the rules and processes of scientific inquiry, they cannot be a part of science."[41]

42. "The annual changes in influenza viruses and the emergence of bacteria resistant to antibiotics are both products of evolutionary forces."[42]

43. "Another example of ongoing evolution is the appearance of mosquitoes resistant to various insecticides, which has contributed to a resurgence of malaria in Africa and elsewhere."[43]

44. "Creationists reject such scientific facts in part because they do not accept evidence drawn from natural processes that they consider to be at odds with the Bible."[44]

45. "To young-earth creationists, no amount of empirical evidence that the earth is billions of years old is likely to refute their claim that the world is actually young but that God simply made it *appear* to be old."[45]

46. "They argue that certain biological structures are so complex that they could not have evolved through processes of undirected mutation and natural selection, a condition they call 'irreducible complexity.' . . . Biologists have examined each of the molecular systems claimed to be the products of design and have shown how they could have arisen through natural processes. For example, in the case of the bacterial flagellum, there is no single, uniform structure that is found in all flagellar bacteria."[46]

47. "The arguments of creationists reverse the scientific process. They begin with an explanation that they are unwilling to alter — that supernatural forces have shaped biological or earth systems —

rejecting the basic requirements of science that hypotheses must be restricted to testable natural explanations."[47]

48. "Their beliefs cannot be tested, modified, or rejected by scientific means and thus cannot be a part of the processes of science."[48]

49. "The pressure to downplay evolution or emphasize nonscientific alternatives in public schools compromises science education."[49]

50. "Despite the lack of scientific evidence for creationist positions, some advocates continue to demand that various forms of creationism be taught together with or in place of evolution in science classes."[50]

51. "Fossils found in rocks of increasing age attest to the interrelated lineage of living things, from the single-celled organisms that lived billions of years ago to *Homo sapiens*."[51]

52. "Even a casual look at different kinds of organisms reveals striking similarities among species, and anatomists have discovered that these similarities are more than skin deep. All vertebrates, for example, from fish to humans, have a common body plan characterized by a segmented body and a hollow main nerve cord along the back. The best available scientific explanation for these common structures is that all vertebrates are descended from a common ancestor species and that they have diverged through evolution."[52]

53. "For example, as described in chapter 3, comparisons of the differences in DNA sequences among organisms provides evidence for many evolutionary events that cannot be found in the fossil record."[53]

54. "Evolution is the only plausible scientific explanation that accounts for the extensive array of observations summarized above."[54]

55. "It is no longer possible to sustain scientifically the view that the living things we see today did not evolve from earlier forms or

that the human species was not produced by the same evolutionary mechanisms that apply to the rest of the living world."[55]

56. "Evolution by natural selection is not only a historical process — it still operates today. For example, the continual evolution of human pathogens has come to pose one of the most serious public health problems now facing human societies."[56]

57. "The creation of a new species from a pre-existing species generally requires thousands of years, so over a lifetime a single human usually can witness only a tiny part of the speciation process."[57]

58. "The best available evidence suggests that life on earth began more than three and a half billion years ago."[58]

59. "Somewhat more than 400 million years ago, some marine plants and animals began one of the greatest of all innovations in evolution — they invaded dry land."[59]

60. "Second, the statements of science should never be accepted as 'final truth.' "[60]

61. "Many teachers are under considerable pressure from policy makers, school administrators, parents, and students to downplay or eliminate the teaching of evolution."[61]

62. "As a result, many U.S. students lack access to information and ideas that are both integral to modern science and essential for making informed, evidence-based decisions about their own lives and our collective future."[62]

63. "Given the importance of science in all aspects of modern life, the science curriculum should not be undermined with nonscientific material."[63]

64. "Several court decisions . . . have ruled that the various forms of creationism, including intelligent design creationism, are religion, not science, and that it is therefore unconstitutional to include them in public school science classes."[64]

65. "If intelligent design creationism were to be discussed in public schools, then Hindu, Islamic, Native American, and other non-Christian creationist views, as well as mainstream religious views that are compatible with science, also should be discussed."[65]

66. "At the same time, many religious people accept the reality of evolution, and many religious denominations have issued emphatic statements reflecting this acceptance."[66]

67. "*Acceptance* of evolution is not the same as a religious *belief.*"[67]

68. "But evolution itself has been so thoroughly tested that biologists are no longer examining *whether* evolution has occurred and is continuing to occur."[68]

69. "Measurements of the radiation left over from the Big Bang also support the universe's great age."[69]

70. "There is no scientific controversy about the basic facts of evolution."[70]

71. "The ideas supported by creationists, in contrast, are not supported by evidence and are not accepted by the scientific community."[71]

72. "Because creationism is based on specific sets of religious convictions, teaching it in science classes would mean imposing a particular religious view on students and thus is unconstitutional, according to several major rulings in federal district courts and the Supreme Court of the United States."[72]

73. [Scientific claims] ". . . should never be accepted as 'final truth.' Nevertheless, in the case of heliocentricism, as in evolution, the data are so convincing that the accuracy of the theory is no longer questioned in science."[73]

74. "Tiny fossils first reveal the existence of bacteria 3.5 to 3.8 billion years ago, and animals composed of more than a single cell are known from about 670 million years ago. But the organisms that lived between these two dates lacked hard parts and, hence, were rarely preserved as fossils."[74]

75. "Scientists believe the earth's age to be about 4.6 billion years because meteorites and rocks of the moon — both of which formed about the same time as the earth — date from this time."[75]

76. "By now, so much evidence has been found that supports the fundamental idea of biological evolution that its occurrence is no longer questioned in science."[76]

77. "The theory of evolution implies that each organism should contain detailed molecular evidence of its relative place in the hierarchy of living things. This evidence can be found in the DNA sequences of living organisms."[77]

78. "Scientists can never be sure that a given explanation is complete and final. Yet many scientific explanations have been so thoroughly tested and confirmed that they are held with great confidence. The theory of evolution is one of these explanations. An enormous amount of scientific investigation has converted what was initially a hypothesis into a theory that is no longer questioned in science."[78]

79. [Evolution] ". . . is no longer questioned in science. . . . One of the most characteristic features of science is this openness to challenge. The willingness to abandon a currently accepted belief when a new, better one is proposed is an important demarcation between science and religious dogma."[79]

80. "Furthermore, because the basic proposals of creation science are not subject to test and verification, these ideas do not meet the criteria for science."[80]

81. "Indeed, U.S. courts have ruled that ideas of creation science are religious views and cannot be taught when evolution is taught."[81]

82. "For example, evidence for a very young earth is incompatible with many different methods of establishing the age of rocks."[82]

83. "Furthermore, many key aspects of evolution occur in relatively short periods that can be observed directly — such as the evolution in bacteria of resistance to antibiotics."[83]

84. "No one saw the evolution of one-toed horses from three-toed horses, but that does not mean that we cannot be confident that horses evolved."[84]

85. "The scientific consensus around evolution is overwhelming."[85]

86. "For example, dinosaurs were extinct long before humans walked the earth. We know this because no human remains have ever been found in rocks dated to the dinosaur era."[86]

87. "Humans did not evolve from modern apes, but humans and modern apes shared a common ancestor, a species that no longer exists. Because we shared a recent common ancestor with chimpanzees and gorillas, we have many anatomical, genetic, biochemical, and even behavioral similarities with the African great apes."[87]

88. "Also, Cambrian fossils did not appear spontaneously. They had ancestors in the Precambrian period, but because these Precambrian forms were soft-bodied, they left fewer fossils."[88]

89. "Usually 'faith' refers to beliefs that are accepted without empirical evidence. . . . If there is a component of faith to science, it is the assumption that the universe operates according to regularities — for example, that the speed of light will not change tomorrow. . . . This 'faith' is very different from religious faith."[89]

Endnotes
1. Peter M.J. Hess, "Science and Religion," 11/25/09, www.ncse.com/religion.
2. Committee on Revising Science and Creationism, *Science, Evolution, and Creationism* (Washington, DC: The National Academies Press, 3rd edition, 2007), p. xi.
3. Ibid., p. xi.
4. Ibid., p. xii.
5. Ibid., p. xiii.
6. Ibid., p. xiii.

7. Ibid., p. 4.
8. Ibid., p. 5.
9. Ibid., p. 11.
10. Ibid., p. 11.
11. Ibid., p. 11.
12. Ibid., p. 12.
13. Ibid., p. 12.
14. Ibid., p. 19.
15. Ibid., p. 20.
16. Ibid., p. 21.
17. Ibid., p. 24.
18. Ibid., p. 26.
19. Ibid., p. 38.
20. Ibid., p. 38.
21. Working Group on Teaching Evolution, NAS, *Teaching about Evolution and the Nature of Science*, (Washington DC: National Academies Press, 1998), p. viii.
22. Ibid., p. viii.
23. Ibid., p. 2.
24. Ibid., p. 2.
25. Ibid., p. 3.
26. Ibid., p. 3.
27. Ibid., p. 3.
28. Ibid., p. 4.
29. Ibid., p. 6.
30. Ibid., p. 7.
31. Ibid., p. 7.
32. Ibid., p. 7.
33. Ibid., p. 8.
34. Ibid., p. 9.
35. Ibid., p. 11.
36. Ibid., p. 11.
37. Ibid., p. 14.
38. Ibid., p. 14.
39. Ibid., p. 15.
40. Ibid., p. 16.
41. *Science, Evolution, and Creationism*, p. 39.
42. Ibid., p. 39.
43. Ibid., p. 39.
44. Ibid., p. 39.
45. Ibid., p. 39.
46. Ibid., p. 40.
47. Ibid., p. 41.
48. Ibid., p. 41.
49. Ibid., p. 43.
50. Ibid., p. 43.
51. *Teaching about Evolution and the Nature of Science*, p. 16.
52. Ibid., p. 16.

53. Ibid., p. 16.
54. Ibid., p. 16.
55. Ibid., p. 16.
56. Ibid., p. 16–17.
57. Ibid., p. 17–18.
58. Ibid., p. 27.
59. Ibid., p. 27.
60. Ibid., p. 30.
61. *Science, Evolution, and Creationism*, p. 43.
62. Ibid., p. 43.
63. Ibid., p. 43.
64. Ibid., p. 44.
65. Ibid., p. 45.
66. Ibid., p. 49.
67. Ibid., p. 49.
68. Ibid., p. 50.
69. Ibid., p. 51.
70. Ibid., p. 52.
71. Ibid., p. 53.
72. Ibid., p. 53.
73. *Teaching about Evolution and the Nature of Science*, p. 30.
74. Ibid., p. 34.
75. Ibid., p. 35.
76. Ibid., p. 39.
77. Ibid., p. 39–40.
78. Ibid., p. 43.
79. Ibid., p. 43.
80. Ibid., p. 55.
81. Ibid., p. 55.
82. Ibid., p. 55.
83. Ibid., p. 55.
84. Ibid., p. 55.
85. Ibid., p. 56.
86. Ibid., p. 57.
87. Ibid., p. 57.
88. Ibid., p. 57.
89. Ibid., p. 58.

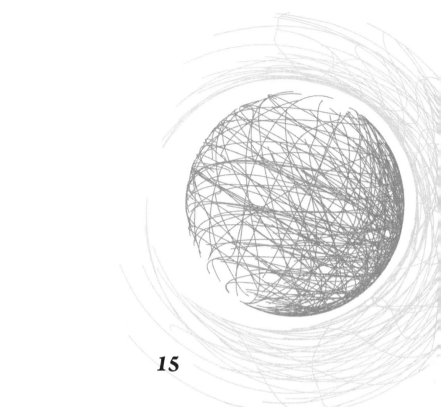

15

Real-world Examples —
Answers

1. **Question-begging Epithet:** "evolution vs. creation*ism*": The "-ism" implies that creation is simply a belief whereas evolution is not, without making an argument for this. ". . . between religion and science": The author uses biased language to equate creation with religion and evolution with science, but no argument is made for this.

2. **Fallacy of False Analogy** and **Equivocation:** Here the author equates science (testable and repeatable operational science in the present) with evolution (the non-testable, non-repeatable belief in molecules-to-man evolution). The analogy is fallacious.

Evolution is not the same kind of "science" as putting men on the moon, so an equivocation is used here as well.

3. **Fallacy of False Cause:** The advances in life sciences are due to scientists studying the continued predictable behavior of the universe, and have not been caused by a belief in evolution in the molecules-to-man sense.

4. **Question-begging Epithet:** The author uses biased language rather than logic to persuade the reader that creation is "non-scientific" and simply a belief. Note the "-ism" attached to "creation" but not "evolution."

5. **Faulty Appeal to Authority** and **Majority:** The implication is that evolution must (or is likely to) be true since most scientists believe it. Even if everyone within the scientific community believed in evolution (which they don't) it wouldn't make it true.

6. **Equivocation** and **Question-begging Epithet:** Creationists do believe in "descent with modification"; that is, organisms do exhibit variation from one generation to the next. But this doesn't prove that all life is descended from one common ancestor, which is the issue in question. So the author has implicitly equivocated on "evolution." The statement that evidence for evolution is "both overwhelming and compelling" is not backed up by anything. It is simply biased language — the question-begging epithet.

7. **Equivocation:** The type of "evolution" (any changes in traits) defined here is not the type of evolution for which the critic is arguing (common descent).

8. **Equivocation** and **Appeal to Fear:** The type of "evolution" referenced here (variation within a kind: virus to virus) is not the type of "evolution" in question (fish to people). The reference to the SARS virus may also be a subtle appeal to fear, implying that not believing in evolution could pose a health risk.

9. **False Analogy:** The theory that the earth orbits the sun is testable and repeatable in the present, unlike the belief in particles-to-people evolution.

10. **Begging the Question:** The author simply states that *Tiktaalik* is an intermediate form between fish and terrestrial animals. But this is an evolutionary assumption — it begs the question.

11. **Begging the Question** and **Question-begging Epithet:** The author here simply assumes that there is abundant evidence for evolution; but this is the very question at issue. He's assuming what he's supposed to be proving. By using biased language to persuade the reader rather than logic (i.e., all the evidence points to evolution, so it would be silly to question it, and the scientists don't), he is committing the question-begging epithet.

12. **False Analogy:** By lumping evolution in with legitimate, well-established sciences, the author hopes the reader will accept evolution by association. However, all the examples provided are operational science, which is testable and repeatable in the present and has supporting evidence. Evolution lacks these things. So the analogy fails.

13. **Faulty Appeal to Authority** and **Appeal to Emotion:** The fact that scientists and theologians believe that evolution can be compatible with faith doesn't necessarily make it so. The "awe and wonder at the history of the universe and life on this planet" are meant to stir an emotional affection for evolution, rather than making a case for it — the appeal to emotion. In fact, evolution is a rather bloody and gruesome mechanism for the explanation of life.

14. **Affirming the Consequent:** Presumably we are meant to draw the conclusion that the big bang must be (or is likely to be) true. But this is invalid. In deductive logic, the syllogism would be stated this way: (1) If the big bang is true, we should expect to detect a cosmic microwave background. (2) We do detect a

cosmic microwave background. (3) Therefore, the big bang is true. This affirms the consequent since there could be many other explanations for the cosmic microwave background.

15. **The Fallacy of Reification:** "According to modern cosmology . . ." implies that "cosmology" can have an opinion on something. It cannot, since it is a concept. It is cosmologists (i.e., people) who have the opinions. But of course, people's opinions are not always right, are always biased (for the better or the worse), and can be diverse. The author may have committed this fallacy to make the argument seem more objective than it really is.

16. **Begging the Question:** That the fossils are tremendously ancient is part of the very claim at issue in the debate. Certainly a biblical creationist would not accept that. The author is subtly assuming part of what he is supposed to be proving.

17. **Begging the Question, Fallacy of False Cause,** and **Affirming the Consequent:** Whether the organisms share common traits because they have a common ancestor or a common Creator is the very question at issue. The author simply assumes his position in arguing for it. Depending on how we fill in this enthymeme, the argument could also be classified as the fallacy of false cause (since creation can also account for similarity) or affirming the consequent: (1) If organisms are descended from a common ancestor, then they would share some traits. (2) They do share some traits. (3) Therefore, they are descended from a common ancestor.

18. **Begging the Question, Fallacy of False Cause,** and **Affirming the Consequent:** This argument is of the same form as the previous one.

19. **Denying the Antecedent:** Putting the enthymeme as a standard mixed hypothetical syllogism, we can see the fallacy: 1. If dinosaurs and humans lived at the same time, then we would find fossils of them in the same layers. 2. We do not find fossils of

them in the same layers. 3. Therefore, they did not live at the same time. But of course, there could be a number of reasons why dinosaur and human fossils (which are somewhat rare, incidentally) are not typically found together.

20. **Begging the Question:** If a mammal fossil were found in sediment that had been estimated to be more than 220 million years old, the estimated age would certainly be changed.

21. **Appeal to Pity:** "Think of the children!" seems to be the message of this argument. That is, if children are not taught evolution, then they are missing essential concepts in science and will be unprepared for the future. This isn't true, of course. But even if it were, it is utterly irrelevant to the topic at issue: whether or not evolution is *true*.

22. **Irrelevant Thesis** and **Faulty Appeal to Authority:** Whether or not the Supreme Court allows creation to be mandated in schools is utterly irrelevant to whether or not it is *true*. Just because the justices believe something doesn't make it so (faulty appeal to authority).

23. **Affirming the Consequent** and **Fallacy of False Cause:** Restating this argument as a deductive syllogism, the fallacy becomes clear: (1) If evolution were true, we'd expect to find similar biochemistry in all life. (2) We do find similar biochemistry in all life. (3) Therefore, evolution is true. But, of course, creationists would also expect to find similar biochemistry in all life, since they share a common Creator, and are designed to live in the same world.

24. **Begging the Question** and **False Cause:** Whether the similarity is due to common ancestry or common design is the very question at issue. The author has simply assumed what he is trying to prove.

25. **Affirming the Consequent:** Presumably we are supposed to draw the conclusion that evolution is true since it can account

for these things. But biblical creation can account for these things, too.

26. **Appeal to Pity:** The phrase "deprives students" is another indication that we are dealing with an emotional approach to persuasion, rather than a logical one.

27. **Equivocation:** Here the author conflates the variation-within-a-kind type of change (which is well-established, testable, and repeatable in the present), with particles-to-people evolution (which has not been observed). By establishing the former, he hopes to persuade people of the latter — a typical "bait and switch."

28. **Faulty Appeal to Authority, Majority, Appeal to Ignorance,** and **Begging the Question:** The majority of people within the scientific community may indeed embrace evolution, but that does not make it so — a faulty appeal to authority/majority. Even if it were the case that there is no evidence against evolution, that would not mean that evolution is true — an appeal to ignorance. Also, the notion that there is no evidence against evolution is very much the issue at hand. The author has begged the question.

29. **Equivocation:** This fallacy centers on the word "evolution." The author uses the "evolution" of the earth (in the sense of "change" in the generic sense) as evidence of "evolution" in the particles-to-people sense.

30. **False Analogy:** Whereas the constitution is highly relevant to civics, the concept of evolution (in the common descent sense) is not at all necessary to understand the science of biology.

31. **Question-begging Epithet:** No logical argument is made. The author simply uses biased language to persuade, e.g., "There really is no debate. Nothing to see here. Move along."

32. **Faulty Appeal to Authority:** The fact that certain organizations have issued public statements about evolution does not make it true.

33. **Equivocation:** The author conflates "evolution" (in the sense of variation within a kind — bacteria becoming resistant) with evolution (in the sense of common descent).

34. **Question-begging Epithet** and **Faulty Appeal to Authority:** This is simply a dismissal of arguments for creation, rather than a logical refutation of them. Since there are many scientists who do embrace good arguments for creation, the author's claim that scientists reject such arguments is a faulty appeal to authority.

35. **Begging the Question:** The author is assuming the validity of the evolutionary worldview when he assigns dates to the fossils; he then uses this as the proof of the evolutionary worldview. This begs the question. Also, the notion that the fossil microorganisms are "primitive" is begging the question.

36. **Begging the Question:** The claim that organisms found lower in the rock strata gradually evolved into organisms found higher in rock strata is the very claim at issue. The author simply assumes an evolutionary relationship between these fossil organisms, and uses this as his argument for an evolutionary relationship between the fossil organisms.

37. **Hasty Generalization:** The fact that mutations are known to cause certain trait variations does not mean that they have caused *all* trait variations.

38. **Affirming the Consequent:** Presumably, this enthymeme is designed to persuade us that evolution must be true. Since the amino acid sequence determines the functionality of the protein, it stands to reason that proteins with nearly identical functions should have very similar amino acid sequences — regardless of their origin. This fact is consistent with either creation or evolution, and so the author has affirmed the consequent.

39. **Affirming the Consequent:** The argument has this basic form: (1) If evolution were true, there would be similarity in the genetic code of all life. (2) There is similarity in the genetic code of all

life. (3) Therefore, evolution is true. The fallacy is obvious when we consider that creationists would *also* expect to find similarity in the genetic code of all life, since all life has the same Creator.

40. **Fallacy of Reification:** Natural selection is a concept. Even though it is a true concept, it cannot literally "test" anything. By reifying natural selection, the author gives it an intellectual ability that it does not truly have, thus sidestepping the issue of why organisms appear to be designed by intelligence.

41. **Special Pleading** and **Irrelevant Thesis:** On the one hand, the author indicates that it is okay to believe in evolution even though it is not directly observable/testable, since inferences from observations are allowed in science. On the other hand, the author indicates that creation is not science since it is not directly observable/testable, but is based on inference from observations. The author has exempted his position from his own standard — special pleading. Also, notice that whether or not creation can be classified as "science" is totally irrelevant to the truth of the position. The author has committed the fallacy of irrelevant thesis.

42. **Equivocation:** The annual changes in influenza viruses never result in anything but influenza viruses. The author conflates this change (within a kind) with evolution in the particles-to-people sense.

43. **Equivocation:** Once again, we see equivocation on the word "evolution." Change within a kind is used as alleged support for changes between kinds.

44. **Strawman Fallacy:** This misrepresents the creationist position. Creationists do not reject any facts (things that are observable/knowable in the present). Rather, biblical creationists interpret facts in light of biblical history.

45. **Strawman Fallacy:** Biblical creationists do not claim that God made the earth "appear" old. "Appearance of age" is an oxymoron since age cannot be seen. Instead, we would contend that

God made the earth fully functioning from the beginning. The evidence today is consistent with an age of thousands of years.

46. **Fallacy of Irrelevant Thesis:** The fact that many different types of flagella exist is not at all relevant to the question at issue. It does not solve the problem of how an apparently irreducibly complex structure could arise through a gradual evolutionary process.

47. **Fallacy of Special Pleading:** Here the author criticizes creationists for their apparent unwillingness to give up the basic interpretive framework (the Bible) in light of which they interpret the evidence. However, evolutionists are also not willing to give up their basic interpretive framework (naturalism) regardless of any evidence to the contrary. The author is using a double standard.

48. **Fallacy of Special Pleading** and **Irrelevant Thesis:** Again, the basic interpretive framework of evolution is naturalism. And most evolutionists are unwilling to consider alternatives. Yet here the author criticizes creationists for doing what he himself does. He is exempting himself from his own standard. Also, whether creation is scientifically testable is not relevant to whether or not it is true.

49. **Question-begging Epithet:** Rather than making a logical argument for evolution, the author simply labels alternatives as "nonscientific." He uses biased language rather than logic to persuade.

50. **Question-begging Epithet:** The author simply states that there is a lack of scientific evidence for creationist positions, rather than arguing for this. Once again, we see "-ism" attached to "creation" but not "evolution," implying that the former is simply a *belief.*

51. **Begging the Question:** The evolutionist claim that living things are all biologically related is supported by the evolutionist claim that rocks have increasing ages spanning billions of years. Since evolution is being used to support evolution, this argument begs

the question. Even if the latter claim were true, it would not prove that one kind is descended from another kind.

52. **Affirming the Consequent** and **Begging the Question:** This argument begs the question since the reason for the similarities among species is the very claim at issue. The arguer simply assumes that such similarities are due to evolution — the very point he is trying to prove. When put into standard form, this argument affirms the consequent; i.e., (1) If evolution is true, there should be similarities. (2) There are similarities. (3) Therefore, evolution is true. But creationists expect such similarities as well.

53. **Affirming the Consequent** and **Begging the Question:** That the similarities in DNA are due to evolution rather than a common creator/common purpose is the very claim at issue. In standard form, this argument commits the fallacy of affirming the consequent, just as the previous one did.

54. **Bifurcation** and **Question-begging Epithet:** The arguer here has implicitly assumed that there are only two options: (1) either evolution explains the data, or (2) there is no explanation. But, since there is a third option (creation), the argument fails. No argument is made for the claim — it is simply an epithet.

55. **Begging the Question:** The idea that "the same evolutionary mechanisms . . . apply to the rest of the living world" is the very point at issue. The arguer has simply assumed evolution to support evolution.

56. **Equivocation:** This is a very clear example of equivocating on the word "evolution." Here, "evolution" in the sense of change within a kind of organism is used as alleged support for particles-to-people evolution. But these are two different concepts.

57. **Begging the Question:** It doesn't occur to the author that perhaps the reason we do not observe evolution (in the particles-to-people sense) today is because it is not true. Instead, he argues

that this must be because evolution happens far too slowly to be observed today. He has assumed evolution in his argument for evolution.

58. **Question-begging Epithet** and **Reification:** Notice that it is the "best" evidence that allegedly supports evolution, yet no support or examples are given. Biased language takes the place of an argument — the fallacy of the question-begging epithet. This argument also contains a mild form of reification, since evidence as a concept cannot actually "suggest" anything. Rather, people make suggestions based on evidence interpreted through their worldview.

59. **Pathetic Fallacy:** Plants and animals are given intelligent characteristics in this example: they are said to begin an "innovation in evolution" by adapting to dry land. This sidesteps the problem of how such design could come about without a designer.

60. **Reification:** Science is a conceptual tool and does not make "statements." Implicitly, the author has also committed the fallacy of special pleading since he has argued earlier that no scientists today seriously question evolution.

61. **Appeal to Pity:** This is meant to stir sympathy for those evolutionists who want to teach evolution in schools, but are being "pressured" by those nasty creationists to not teach evolution. However, most creationists want evolution to be taught in schools — as long as the problems with evolution are not hidden from the students.

62. **Appeal to Pity:** This is another "think of the children" type argument where we are supposed to feel sympathy for the poor deprived students who allegedly won't be able to make good life decisions if they are not taught evolution.

63. **Question-begging Epithet:** Without making an actual argument, the author simply implies that alternatives to evolution are nonscientific.

64. **Fallacy of Irrelevant Thesis:** Whether or not creation is classified as religion or science by the courts is totally irrelevant to whether or not it is true. There is also a subtle appeal to force fallacy in this argument — i.e., "if you teach creation, you might be sued" seems to be implied.

65. **Slippery Slope Fallacy:** The author suggests that discussing intelligent design or creation in schools will lead to the chain of events whereby the creation views of many other religions must be discussed as well. This isn't likely since most other religions embrace some form of evolution anyway. So there is a false analogy here as well. A subtle question-begging epithet also occurs here: "as well as mainstream religious views that are compatible with science" implies that creationists are a fringe community and that creation is not compatible with science — but no argument has been made for this.

66. **Faulty Appeal to Authority** and **Question-begging Epithet:** The fact that many people believe in evolution and that many denominations have issued such statements is totally irrelevant to whether or not evolution is *true*. Also, "accept the reality of evolution" is a question-begging epithet, since whether or not evolution is reality is the very claim at issue.

67. **Special Pleading:** This one is subtle. Here the author is trying to exempt himself from the fact that he too has beliefs that color his interpretation of the evidence. He has a double standard. We might very well respond, "If that is so, then I don't have a religious *belief* in creation, I simply *accept* it."

68. **Question-begging Epithet:** No argument is presented. The author simply uses biased language to persuade the reader that evolution is unquestionable.

69. **Begging the Question:** Whether the microwave background radiation is from the big bang or something else is the very question at issue. The author assumes the big bang is true, in order

to argue that the radiation allegedly produced by it supports the big bang. He is assuming what he is trying to prove.

70. **Question-begging Epithet:** No argument is made. The author simply asserts that evolution is true using biased language to persuade.

71. **Begging the Question** and **Faulty Appeal to Authority:** The author merely assumes that the evidence does not support creation in order to argue against creation. But this is the very point at issue. He then appeals to the scientific community in support for evolution. But even if every member of the scientific community believed in evolution (which is not the case), it wouldn't make it so.

72. **Special Pleading, Irrelevant Thesis,** and **Appeal to Authority:** Whether or not creation is based on religious beliefs or is unconstitutional are both irrelevant to the *truth* of the position — so this is an irrelevant thesis. Also, evolution is also based on a religious/philosophical view: naturalism. So the author has exempted himself from the same standard (special pleading). The reference to the Supreme Court is an irrelevant appeal to authority.

73. **False Analogy** and **Special Pleading:** The author has linked heliocentricism (which is observable and testable in the present) with particles-to-people evolution (which is not observable/testable in the present), so this is a false analogy. The author also has a double standard: on the one hand, scientific claims should never be accepted as final truth, but on the other hand, evolution is no longer questioned.

74. **Begging the Question** and **Appeal to Ignorance:** The estimated ages of such fossils are based on the evolutionary worldview; yet they are used in support of the evolutionary worldview. Also, the supposed transitional forms are said to have soft parts that do not fossilize well, which is allegedly why there is no evidence of their existence — an appeal to ignorance.

75. **Begging the Question:** The estimated evolutionary age of the earth is based on an evolutionary interpretation of radiometric dating of moon rocks, which allegedly formed at the same time as the earth in the evolution worldview.

76. **Question-begging Epithet:** Yet, no such evidence is presented, only evidence that makes just as much sense in a biblical creation worldview.

77. **Affirming the Consequent:** Essentially the argument is: (1) If evolution, then hierarchy in DNA. (2) There is hierarchy in DNA. (3) Therefore, evolution is true. But creation scientists also expect such a hierarchy, since God has made it possible for us to classify living things.

78. **Special Pleading:** On the one hand, scientists can never be sure. On the other hand, evolution is allegedly no longer questioned (i.e., we can be sure about it) — an inconsistent double standard.

79. **Special Pleading:** On the one hand, evolution is said to be no longer questioned in science. On the other hand, one of the most characteristic features of science is openness to challenge. The author is apparently exempting his own view from this criterion.

80. **Fallacy of Irrelevant Thesis:** Whether or not creation can be classified as "science" is totally irrelevant to whether it is true.

81. **Faulty Appeal to Authority:** The rulings of U.S. courts on whether or not creation science is a religious view and whether or not it can be taught in public schools has no bearing on the *truth* of creation.

82. **Begging the Question:** Since such methods are based on old-earth assumptions (i.e., uniformitarianism), the author has merely assumed what he is trying to prove. This is arbitrary and reversible. We could equally well say that evidence for an old earth is incompatible with all those methods that establish a young age for the earth.

83. **Equivocation:** As usual, the equivocation occurs on the word "evolution," which is used in the particles-to-people sense, and then switched to the adaptation-within-a-kind sense (bacteria resistance).

84. **Appeal to Ignorance** and **Equivocation:** The lack of observational evidence against horse "evolution" is taken as evidence for horse evolution. Also, the type of "evolution" involved seems to all be within the horse kind, and is thus not evolution in the molecules-to-man sense. This is the fallacy of equivocation.

85. **Faulty Appeal to Authority/Majority:** The opinion of the majority of scientists does not prove the claim at issue.

86. **Denying the Antecedent:** The formal argument is: (1) If dinosaur and human fossils were found together, then they lived at the same time. (2) They are not found together. (3) Thus, they did not live at the same time.

87. **Begging the Question** and **False Cause:** The reason why we share some anatomical features with animals (common ancestor or common Creator) is the very question at issue.

88. **Appeal to Ignorance** and **Begging the Question:** The reason we do not find certain transitional forms is because they didn't exist. Yet the evolutionist takes such a lack of evidence and points out that if they were soft-bodied then they would leave no evidence — which begs the question.

89. **Strawman Fallacy:** Biblical faith is not belief without evidence. Rather, biblical faith is the confidence we have in the self-attesting Word of God, which is confirmed by evidence. It is not a blind faith.

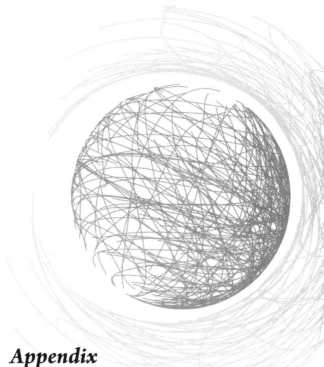

Appendix

Alternate Names of Fallacies Including Latin Names (in Italics)

The appeal to emotion: *argumentum ad populum*

The appeal to force: *argumentum ad baculum*

The appeal to ignorance: *argumentum ad ignorantiam*

The appeal to pity: *argumentum ad misericordiam*

Begging the question: *petito principii*

Complex question: *plurium interrogationum*

Equivocation: "bait and switch"

Fallacy fallacy: *Argumentum ad logicam,* "argument to logic"

Fallacy of false cause: *non causa pro causa*
(subclass 1): "After this, therefore because of this": *post hoc ergo propter hoc*
(subclass 2): "With this, therefore because of this": *cum hoc ergo propter hoc*

Faulty appeal to authority: Appeal to Inappropriate/Improper Authority, *argumentum ad verecundiam*

Hasty generalization: the fallacy of converse accident, *a dicto secundum quid ad dictum simpliciter*

Irrelevant thesis: irrelevant conclusion, red herring, *ignoratio elenchi*

Reification: hypostatization, or the fallacy of misplaced concretion
(subclass): the pathetic fallacy

Slippery slope fallacy: absurd extrapolation

Sweeping generalization: the fallacy of accident, *a dicto simpliciter ad dictum secundum quid* (sometimes simplified to: *dicto simpliciter*)

"to the man": *ad hominem*
(subclass): "poisoning the well"

Glossary

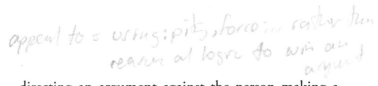

Ad Hominem — directing an argument against the person making a claim rather than the claim itself.

Affirming the Consequent — an argument where the second premise affirms the consequent of the first premise.

Appeal to Emotion — fallacy of attempting to persuade people by stirring powerful emotions rather than making a logical case.

Appeal to Force/Fear — arguing for a position on the basis that negative consequences will follow if a person does not accept the position.

Appeal to Ignorance — fallacy of appealing to the unknown; specifically when a person argues that a claim is probably true simply because it has never been proven false.

Appeal to Pity — persuading people to accept a position by generating sympathy for those who hold the position.

Begging the Question — merely assuming what one is attempting to prove.

Bifurcation — claiming there are only two mutually exclusive possibilities, when there may actually be three or more options.

Complex Question — attempting to persuade by asking a loaded question.

Denying the Antecedent — an argument where the second premise denies the antecedent of the first premise.

Equivocation — shifting from one meaning of a word to another within an argument.

"Fallacy" Fallacy — assuming that a claim is false simply because an argument for that position is fallacious.

Fallacy of Composition — arguing that what is true of the parts must also be true of the whole, or what is true of the members of a group is also true of the group.

Fallacy of Division — arguing that what is true of the whole must also be true of the parts.

Fallacy of False Cause — attributing a false cause-and-effect relationship between two events.

Fallacy of Irrelevant Thesis — proving a point, but not the point at issue.

False Analogy — making a comparison between two things that are alike in only trivial ways, irrelevant to the argument.

Faulty Appeal to Authority — endorsing a claim simply based on the person making it.

Formal Fallacies — mistakes in reasoning stemming from the structure (the form) of the argument.

Genetic Fallacy — dismissing an argument because one objects to the source of the argument. *own merits*

Hasty Generalization — drawing a generalization from too few specific examples.

Hypothetical Proposition — a proposition stating that if part A is true, then part B must be true as well.

Mixed Hypothetical Syllogism — an argument with two premises, only one of which is hypothetical.

Moralistic Fallacy — asserting that because something should be a particular way, it is a particular way. *should change*

Naturalistic Fallacy — arguing that since something is a particular way, it is morally acceptable for it to be that way. *— should remain*

"No True Scotsman" Fallacy — when an arguer defines a term in a biased way to protect his argument from rebuttals.

arbitrary Ⓟ

Question-begging Epithet — using biased (often emotional) language to persuade people rather than using logic.

Reification — attributing a concrete characteristic to something abstract.

Slippery Slope Fallacy — arguing that a particular action will set off an undesirable chain of events, when in reality other factors would tend to prevent such a result.

Special Pleading — fallacy of applying a double standard.

Strawman Fallacy — misrepresenting an opponent's position and proceeding to refute the misrepresentation rather than what the opponent actually claims.

Sweeping Generalization — applying a generalization to an exception.

exceptions
anomalies
atypical
exclusive
established

unjustified assumption
arbitrary assumption / definition

J ason Lisle is a research scientist and speaker with Answer in Genesis Ministries. He holds a bachelor's degree in physics and astronomy from Ohio Wesleyan University, and a master's degree and Ph.D. in astrophysics from the University of Colorado in Boulder. Dr. Lisle is also the planetarium director at the Creation Museum, and has written several of the programs now available, including "The Created Cosmos" and "Worlds of Creation."

Dr. Lisle has written extensively on the topics of creation and astronomy, in secular and creation literature. He is author of the book *The Ultimate Proof of Creation*, and is a co-author of *The New Answers Book*, volumes I, II, and III. For more information on Dr. Lisle, including his speaking schedule and information on the latest planetarium shows at the Creation Museum, visit www.answersingenesis.org.

An argument for Creation
that **cannot be denied**

An exceptional book for pastors, ministry leaders,
seminary attendees, and students of religion and philosophy

- Shows how to understand the nature of scientific evidence and how it is interpreted

- Discusses worldviews, and the relationship between a person's worldview and evidence

- Reveals the truth of biblical creation, the Bible in general, the existence of God, and the foundational aspects of Christianity

Master Books®
A Division of New Leaf Publishing Group
www.masterbooks.net

6 x 9 • 256 pages
paperback • $13.99
ISBN-13: 978-0-89051-568-6

Dr. Lisle says there is an argument that demonstrates that the Christian worldview must be true, and thus, biblical creation must be true as well since it is an integral part of the Christian worldview. It is powerful, conclusive, and has no possible rebuttal, and as such, it is an irrefutable argument — an "ultimate proof" of the Christian worldview.

Available at Christian booksellers nationwide or at www.nlpg.com

VITAL EVIDENCE:

- Abundant biblical, theological, and scientific evidence to demonstrate the importance of scriptural authority.

- Why this is a critical issue to the Church, its survival, and its relevance.

- The Church's changing interpretations of Scripture.

- How the Bible is used by both young-earth and old-earth creationists to support their position.

Master Books®
A Division of New Leaf Publishing Group
www.masterbooks.net

5.5 x 8.5 • 240 pages
Paperback • $12.99
ISBN-13: 978-0-89051-544-0

THE VERDICT IS IN

"Twenty-somethings once faithfully attended church. What made them stop? While most said they still believe that the Bible is God's Word, they also said that the idea that the earth is millions of years old was one thing that caused them to doubt the Bible. . . . The crumbling foundation of the Church takes a devastating toll on future generations. Therefore, churches must reclaim the historical truth found in Genesis and apply the Bible's authority to every area of life."

— Ken Ham, President
Answers in Genesis

*Available at Christian bookstores nationwide
or at www.nlpg.com*

A Comprehensive Guide to the Heavens

"This book is meant to be an introduction only — a starting point to a biblical view of the universe. . . . Who knows what amazing truths are waiting to be discovered if only the shackles of secular thinking are removed. Now is the time of discovery. . . ."

7 x 9 • Hardcover
128 pages • $15.99
Full color interior
ISBN: 978-089051-471-9

Master Books®
A Division of New Leaf Publishing Group
www.masterbooks.net

Available at local Christian booksellers nationwide or at www.nlpg.com.

With a doctorate in astrophysics from the University of Colorado, Dr. Jason Lisle is your guide to the universe beyond our world in this remarkable book.

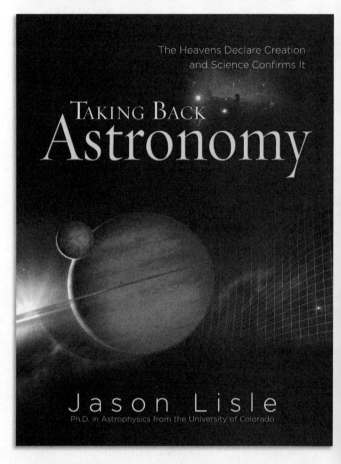

The Heavens Declare Creation and Science Confirms It

TAKING BACK
Astronomy

Jason Lisle
Ph.D. in Astrophysics from the University of Colorado

Taking Back Astronomy is filled with facts that challenge secular theories and models of the universe — how it began and how it continues to amaze the scientific community. This book explores numerous evidences that point to a young universe: magnetic poles of planets, the spiral shape of galaxies, comets, and more. It explains the scale and size of the universe — something that is hard for our minds to imagine. With over 50 color photos of rarely seen stars, nebulas, and galaxies, Dr. Lisle guides you out among the stars to experience the awesome power of God's vast creation.

Join the
Conversation

Ask the experts

Build relationships

Share your thoughts

Download free resources

Creation
Conversations
.com

This is your invitation to our
online community of believers.